Phil & Bridgette,
Thanks for
interest. I hope
this work adds value
to your life.

God bless,
Mark

What Reviewers are Saying

"What a perfectly fun, reflective, and inspirational piece. Having worked with Maxie for several years, I've really come to appreciate his unique way of expressing the world around him. I'm pleased to have more of his material from which to draw. I'm now going to "stick a fork in it, I think I'm done."
>—Coleman Peterson, Executive Vice President, People Division, Wal-Mart Stores, Inc.

"Maxie has written a fresh new reference of unusual quotes and phrases that have special meaning for everyday business and personal life. They cause you to stop and think about things in ways that are, as his work suggests, "simple and relevant." He's done it with a refreshing new format that enhances your understanding and influences how you communicate with others. Whether you refer to it each morning with a few pages as you drink your first cup of coffee, or conclude each evening with a few reminders in preparation for the next day's conversations, you will find this book an invaluable resource for any situation."
>—Don Soderquist, former Executive Vice President & CEO, Wal-Mart Stores, Inc., Founder & Executive in Residence, Soderquist Center for Leadership & Ethics

"Maxie Carpenter has written the book I've been looking for. For years he has collected the best of the best message phrases. They are amazing "axioms for the good life." One of my favorites is: "Hats off to the past, coats off to the future."

His wit and wisdom are drawn from every quarter of life and from a broad spectrum of wizened contributors. In addition, his commentary about each phrase lends even more strength to his impressive book. Congratulations Maxie!"
>—Dr. Paul Faulkner Ph.D., Author, Founder & President, Resources for Living, Inc.

"Down-home wisdom from the heart. Thought-provoking and inspirational. Deceivingly simple with deep messages."
—Roger E. Herman, Certified Management Consultant, Author

"In a busy world we seldom have time to read those things which would benefit us most. Maxie Carpenter has created the ideal format. You can start at almost any page in this book and within five minutes accumulate several ideas which will influence what you are doing and what you will do".
—Dave Yoho, President, Dave Yoho Associates Counsultants, Author of *How To Have A Great Year Every Year* and *Power Linguistics*

"This book can help you grow in business and in life . . ."

—Nido Qubein, CSP, CPAE Chairman of four companies, Speaks on Transformational Leadership and Positioning

"If you want to be inspired...day after day...with only a few minutes at a time, this book is a must read. It will enrich your life!"
—Hal Becker, CSP, The Becker Group Author of *Can I have 5 Minutes of Your Time* and *Lip Service*

"A tremendous book of wisdom, humor and love. Read just one page and your day will be inspired. This is one book you will re-read many times."
Charles 'Tremendous' Jones, CPAE Author of *Life is Tremendous*

"An inspiring tribute to family and the burning desire to achieve"
—David Alan CEO, MAIL-RITE INTERNATIONAL INC. Author of *The $100 Million Dollar Playbook*

I Didn't Ask You to Dance!
I Asked You to Talk!

A commonsense, humorous,
and at times, spiritual approach
to communication in a generation
obsessed with political correctness.

Maxie Carpenter

Oakhill Press
Winchester, Virginia

Reproduction or translation of any part of this work beyond that permitted by Section 107 or 108 of the 1976 United States Copyright Act without the permission of the copyright owner is unlawful. Requests for permission or further information should be addressed to the Permissions Department, Oakhill Press.

This publication is designed to provide accurate and authoritative information in regard to the subject matter covered. It is sold with the understanding that the publisher is not engaged in rendering legal, accounting, or other professional service. If legal advice or other expert assistance is required, the services of a competent professional person should be sought. *From a Declaration of Principles jointly adopted by a committee of the American Bar Association and a committee of publishers.*

Without limiting the rights under copyright reserved above, no part of this publication may be reproduced, stored in or introduced into a retrieval system, or transmitted, in any form or by any means (electronic, mechanical, photocopying, recording, or otherwise) without the prior written permission of the publisher of this book.

The author and publisher express their sincere gratitude to all people quoted herein. Every effort has been made to find the proper origin of quoted material. If by oversight anything in this book has been quoted erroneously or misattributed, proper acknowledgment will be made in future printings after notice has been received.

10   9   8   7   6   5   4   3   2   1

Book design and production by Bookwrights Design
Jacket design by Michael Komarck
Printed in the United States of America

Library of Congress Cataloging-in-Publication Data

Carpenter, Maxie, 1950-
  I didn't ask you to dance! I asked you to talk! : a common sense, humorous, and at times spiritual approach to communication in a world obsessed with political correctness / by Maxie Carpenter.
    p. cm.
Includes bibliographical references.
ISBN 1-886939-62-4 (alk. paper)
  1. Communication in management. 2. Leadership—Moral and ethical aspects. 3. Business ethics. I Title.

HD30.3.C356 2004
658.4'5--dc22   2004053187

Oakhill Press
1647 Cedar Grove Road
Winchester, VA 22603
800-32-books

DEDICATION

To the memory of my father,
John Mack Carpenter,
the best "people guy" I ever knew.
—Maxie Carpenter

The author and his father

I've never considered myself a student of higher learning, and at the age of fifty-three, I'm still trying to obtain a degree. However, from the time I left college in 1973 to begin my career with Wal-Mart, until December 8, 1996, when my father passed, it's always been one of my goals. I regret not being able to accomplish that before Dad was gone. Though he never attended college, I know he was proud of me, and I'm thankful for his influence upon my life. When I finally get that degree, I'll visit him at his resting place in good-old Ash Flat, Arkansas, and tell him all about it.

For me, Dad was a case study in man's ability to communicate with a true heart for people, which is a very rare gift. Hardly a week passes that I don't have occasion to speak to at least one person, whether by coincidence, intention, or otherwise, who doesn't mention my father and how he influenced their life in some way.

So, here's to my dad, an ordinary man who, with nothing more than a high school education, lived it, learned it, survived it, thrived in it, and through his family and friends, accomplished extraordinary things and left a legacy and philosophy about life that still remains alive today.

Contrary to popular opinion, one size does not fit all when it comes to communicating with people.

—Maxie Carpenter

Contents

Foreword

People, in general, want to be told the truth, and they want the truth communicated to them in an effective, straightforward, and trustworthy manner. Why? Because they want to be acknowledged, respected for their contributions, make informed decisions, and be involved. They want to be involved in the governmental process, the corporate process, the non-profit process, the educational process, the religious process and any other basic life process.

If we look at the way the current presidential campaign is being communicated, it's easy to understand why we have the largest electorate in history still undecided about who will get their vote. They're simply not sure whether they have accurate information.

If we look at the way corporate America is communicating their financial performance, it's easy to understand why we have the largest majority of investors in history undecided about where they will invest their future. They're simply not sure whether they have accurate information.

If we look at the way non-profits communicate to contributors about how their money is being appropriately channeled to those in need, it's easy to understand why the largest number of donors in history are hesitant about their levels of giving. They're simply not sure whether they have accurate information.

If we look at how public education inconsistently communicates student progress, it's easy to understand why more parents than ever before don't know whether they're children are making the grade or not. They're simply not sure whether they have accurate information.

If we look at the way the religious community rationalizes shifts in philosophy that defy biblical scripture, traditional beliefs, and constitutional standards regarding separation of church and state, it's easy to understand why we have the largest percentage of the population in history confused about their spirituality. They're not sure whether they have accurate information.

Maxie Carpenter doesn't provide solutions for how to correct any of these situations. If he did, aside from the bible, this might be the best selling publication in history. What he does provide is a collection of experiences that clearly illustrate a philosophy of communication that is influenced by empathy and concern for the individual rather than the pursuit of an agenda. His simplicity and relevance is compelling because it translates to each and every one of us, regardless of what or who we're involved with. Enjoy it with my compliments

Charlie "Tremendous" Jones
CPAE and author of *Life is Tremendous*

Acknowledgments

I'd like to thank my wife, Brenda, and my kids, Micah (fifteen) and Shelby (thirteen), for their love and patience as this effort was being completed. They've watched their husband and father work at various endeavors of a charitable and spiritual nature, all the while trying to decide what he wanted to do with his second life. Basically, after a twenty-seven-year career with Wal-Mart, I think I've been growing up all over again.

I'd like to thank Bill and Susan for an enduring friendship. They've helped me more than they know to understand that it's not the most important thing in the world to have an agenda all the time. It's more important to feel better about yourself than it is to worry about how others feel about you. I'd also like to thank Bryan for continually encouraging me to realize that I'm a better professional than I thought I was.

I'd like to honor and praise the Lord for providing for my family, even during those times when we didn't know He was there. One of my favorite verses in the Bible is Joshua 24:15. This scripture is a reminder that no matter how many goals, activities, missions, purposes, desires, or expectations a person fills their daily life with, it all comes down to one question: What is the ultimate purpose for our presence on this earth? **That purpose, simply stated, is to serve.** Regardless of what we may find ourselves involved in, whether private or public, spiritual or secular, our mission is simply to serve others in as Christ-like a manner as possible.

> *"But if you are unwilling to serve the Lord, then choose today whom you will serve. Would you prefer the gods of your ancestors served beyond the Euphrates? Or will it be the gods of the Amorites in whose land you now live?* ***But, as for me and my house, we will serve the Lord!"***
> Joshua 24:15 (author's emphasis)

We're faced with choices every day of our lives. We're continually challenged relative to the path we choose for our lives to take, and we continually affirm the choices we make in some way. In my opinion, it's much easier and more fulfilling to affirm the right choices than the wrong ones.

> *It's easy to slip into a quiet rebellion where you go about your own way. But the time always comes when you have to choose who or what will control you. The choice is yours. Will it be the Lord, your own limited personality, or an imperfect substitute?*
>
> *Life Application Study Bible*
> (Wheaton, IL: Tyndale House Publishers, 1996)

Please turn to the back of the book for more acknowledgments.

Introduction

We live in an age where the art of communication has become the art of spin control. Every medium known to man, from a newspaper to a computer, has become a tool of influence to move the masses to believe or disbelieve. From the local school board to the highest office in the land, those in positions of leadership communicate with those who hold them accountable, in the hope that they will be perceived as credible, sincere, and caring. When the behavior doesn't reflect the commitment, the need for spin control becomes necessary, and the public falls prey to an onslaught of denials, affirmations, betrayals, admissions, and cries for support, forgiveness, and understanding.

The art of spin control is also used by people in the private and corporate workplace to communicate verbally with their supervisors, peers, or others under their supervision. It may take place in a counseling session, a public presentation, a grassroots meeting, a business meeting, or a personal conversation. It may serve the purpose of avoiding the real issue, confusing the participants, diverting attention from the agenda, giving a false impression of intelligence, or providing an opportunity to run for office. Whatever the circumstance or motive, spin control is too often a form of communication that can be very frustrating to those who do not want to hear a politically correct response. Many people simply want to be talked to in a manner they can clearly understand.

People don't respond in ways you expect, until they know how much you care about them. During my thirty-one years of managing people, both inside and outside the workplace, my experience has been that people want only two things from other people: They want to be listened to with understanding and responded to in ways they understand. There's not one single discussion that people have about compensation, a career path, a coaching, an appraisal outcome, or a personal issue that doesn't require those two activities. The most effective way to communicate with any of our professional or personal partners, whether in private or in public, is to listen with sincerity and empathy and respond in the same manner.

It's also been my experience that a sense of humor is one of the most beneficial personality traits you can possess. It can break the ice, blunt hostility, temper nervousness, reveal the human side, and more importantly, simplify the message. A sense of humor has personally helped me to realize that life is not to be lived every day as if it were an emergency.

Over the years, I've been taking note of what I'll call message phrases: one-or two-sentence phrases that, in their simplicity, clearly convey a message one person may be trying to communicate to another. These statements are born out of my own experiences, those I've picked up from partners in the workplace, those I've picked up from family and friends outside the workplace, those I've taken from the writings of many authors I've read and admired, and many taken from simply listening to the myriad of conversations conducted by people around us every day that reflect the experience of their lives. This book records these message phrases and my interpretation of or commentary on them. No matter who you are or what your chosen profession, if you read far enough, something in here has an application for just about anyone.

Additionally, I trust you'll notice the references to many historical people, even as far back as 604 BC. This is a result of two influences. First, my favorite subject was always history, and I continue to marvel as I come across some of the amazing people and events that have changed the course of our lives and the history of the world. Second, I feel we've too often abandoned the traditions, wisdom, vision, and culture of our past for the sake of a future that is being influenced more by what is politically correct than by what is morally right.

An acute empathy for how people feel, along with a sense of humor, have helped me recognize that people only want to hear the truth, regardless of how it may make them feel. They also want to hear it in a simple, caring, straightforward manner. I hope you enjoy this collection of life, and that the reading of it will add some value to your daily efforts to navigate an environment that challenges all of us, both professionally and spiritually.

CHAPTER ONE

Taking Responsibility

I've always found it surprising how people, in general, are unwilling to take responsibility for the choices they make. It seems there's always someone else to blame or some set of circumstances that are beyond one's control, other than simply the personal choice of the individual.

—Maxie Carpenter

The author, his mother, and his sisters

When my father was away on business, I was responsible. One of the rites of passage that I think a lot of the young men of today's generation miss going through is one where an authority figure (traditionally the father) passes on a sense of responsibility that marks a crossing over into manhood. Such a process defines that sense of responsibility in terms of personal ownership, personal acceptance, and personal accountability that doesn't allow for rationalization, blame-shifting, substitution, alternative choice, external negative influences, or political maneuvering. It's also a process that clearly defines where the boundaries are, how much authority is available, what the terms of engagement are, and who's ultimately responsible. In my case, I knew the buck stopped with me. That lesson would be invaluable.

Phrase	Message
If there's no consequence, what's the point of doing anything? 　　　　　　—mc	People should understand that every action has a re-action. It can be a reward for accomplishment or a penalty for lack of trying.
If you want to be success-ful, go do the tough stuff. If you want to be comfort-able, "homesteading" is the only way to go. 　　　　　　—mc	I talk to people every day who can't seem to under-stand why their careers have stalled out. When we talk about moving to where the opportunity is, the con-versation stalls out too.
There are victims, and then there are volunteers. You have a choice. 　　　　　　—mc	The only victims I know are children and those in elder care. When we stop making excuses for our failures, we can start learn-ing from them and turn them into successes.

The tongue weighs practically nothing, yet so few can hold it.

—unknown

The most difficult individual to hold accountable for the communicating of knowledge, whether personal or public, is oneself. A certain amount of character, professionalism, and integrity is required to decide what is appropriate to discuss, whether to have the dicussion, how to have the discussion, and with whom to have the discussion.

"The greatest crime in the world is not developing your potential. When you do what you do best, you are helping others."

—Roger Williams (1603–1683), governor of Newport Colony

The truest form of cheating is that of denying yourself the opportunity to exploit your talents to the ultimate degree. To leave this life without knowing how great you could have become is truly a crime.

"My interest is in the future, because I'm going to spend the rest of my life there."

—Charles Kettering (1876–1958), inventor

Constantly looking back and allowing the past to influence your willingness to embrace change will stunt any growth or success you may want to achieve.

People don't usually forget what they've learned. They just choose to stop using it.
　　　　　　　　　—mc

Personal choice will always determine the degree of responsibility one is willing to recognize or disregard.

"The most underutilized leadership trait today is curiosity. It's that natural tinker's mentality that spells the difference between par and world class."
　　　　　—Jimmy Wright,
　　　　　founding partner,
　　　　　Diversified Retail
　　　　　Solutions, LLC

The very best leaders always want to know what, who, why, how, and when on a continual basis.

Too many leaders practice the timeless art of "convenient amnesia" in an attempt to avoid taking responsibility for the decisions they make.
　　　　　　　　　—mc

There is no better way to destroy your credibility in the shortest amount of time than to pretend you forgot. That excuse not only causes people to lose respect for you, it actually breeds contempt because of the lack of integrity you display.

"Follow through, don't fall through."
—Keith Aubele, founder, Acclaim Management Group

One of the most significant traits exhibited by successful leaders is the art of following through. It's the attention to detail that separates those who achieve the pinnacle from those who only make it to the first or second tier.

"If you don't get better every year, then you should probably lose your job."
—Mike Irwin, Sports Talk Radio 1190 AM, Fayetteville, Arkansas

The formula for endurance in the job market is pretty simple, isn't it?

"Hold yourself to a higher standard than others expect of you."
—Henry Ward Beecher (1813–1887), American clergyman

It's easy to know the standard required when you have only yourself to compare to. It's when you compare yourself to others that you know whether or not your personal standard was high enough.

CHAPTER TWO

Environmental Influence

In today's professional environment, there is often such a focus on the business at hand—sales, expense control, profit, growth, etc.—that it becomes too convenient to ignore the talents, needs, and contributions of those who are held accountable for those elements of that business.

—Maxie Carpenter

The author's father (left) and uncles

My father and his two brothers were all in the service as part of the occupational force in Germany after World War II. This picture was taken during a family reunion at Blowing Springs Park located in Bella Vista, Arkansas. My uncle Hayden, sitting in the middle, had a career as a line manager in a Libby's plant in California.

The brother on the right, my uncle Boyd, was a county judge, state representative, and bank president in Sharp County in Northeast Arkansas. My father held many jobs, all the way from a service station owner and operator in Hardy, Arkansas, to a real estate salesman in Benton County in Northwest Arkansas, which turned into his chosen profession and a thirty-five-year career. They were all bigger than life to me at times as I was growing up, and were all tremendously influential in shaping my perspectives because they were men of influence in their families, their professions, and their communities.

Phrase	Message
The only ones who didn't commit any turnovers were the ones who didn't get to play. —mc	Never assume that those around you don't have the capacity to learn more than what they're currently contributing. The best companies in the world exploit the talents of their people by exposing them to areas of the business that are outside their comfort zones.
"Some of the best things in life aren't things." —Joann Davis, author	The best thing in life is life itself.

"It's human nature to think about ourselves. It's human relations to think about others."
—Bob Moawad, chairman/ CEO, Edge Learning Institute

Really great leaders always think of others first and display that character trait by example and without fail, continuously.

"Do exactly as I tell you, or you'll never play again!"
—A junior high basketball coach

This is a self-fulfilling prophecy because people, in general, do exactly what you tell them to do. How often you tell them the same thing influences their ability to do more than you expect of them.

"As an organization grows, it must become more human, not less."
—Swift & Co. corporate principle, 1920

Anything worth accomplishing can only be realized through people. If you don't value that philosophy, then your chances of surviving for an extended period of time are very limited.

"It's fine to have ability, but the ability to discover ability in others is the true test."
—Elbert Hubbard (1856– 1915), editor; author; founder, Roycrofters

People put you where they want you based entirely upon how they feel about you, and how they feel about you is based entirely upon how much time you invest in them.

The greatest good we can do for others is not to share our riches, but to reveal theirs.

—unknown

Great is the leader who continually looks for greatness in others for the purpose of lifting them up in the organization.

"This is a team effort. If you can't put people up, please don't put them down."

—NASA slogan

This simple statement puts forth a relevant core value that any person or organization should clearly understand and support.

"You can work miracles by having faith in others. To get the best out of people, choose to think and believe the best about them."

—Bob Moawad, chairman/ CEO, Edge Learning Institute

No one gets up every day and comes to work with the intention of doing everything they can to ruin your life. Don't be trapped into thinking they do.

"When building a team, I always search for people who love to win. If I can't find any of those, I look for people who hate to lose."

—H. Ross Perot, billionaire; Reform Party founder; presidential candidate, 1992, 1996

When you want to hire people really badly, you usually hire really bad people. Don't compromise your standards for the sake of urgency.

"People tend to resist that which is forced upon them and tend to support that which they helped create."
—Vince Plaff, communications consultant

People who feel ownership in an initiative will live and die for it.

"Sometimes, influence is not what you are but what you appear to be."
—Lolan Mackey, founding partner, Diversified Retail Solutions, LLC

Today's business environment is playing host to the trend in casual wear, and that may even be appropriate to some degree. Regardless, just remember that appearance is reality.

"Resentment is incompatible with success. Always be the first to forgive and then be the first to forgive yourself."
—Dan Zadra, author, publisher, strategic communications consultant

Forgiveness is the one character trait most admired by the masses and least practiced by leadership.

"Hire the best, pay them fairly, communicate frequently, provide challenges and rewards, believe in them, and get out of their way. They'll knock your socks off."
—Mary Ann Allison, author, lecturer, consultant

This formula works every time almost without exception. Why so few use it is beyond my imagination.

"Celebrate what you want to see more of."
Tom Peters, writer, speaker, consultant

In today's economy, the pace is so fast that little time remains to celebrate your victories because they seem so few and far between. But celebrate them you must, because your partners won't allow you to hang around for very long if you don't.

"Never doubt that a small group of thoughtful committed citizens can change the world; indeed, it is the only thing that ever has."
—Margaret Meade (1901–1978), anthropologist

When your mind's made up, it doesn't take much to cause a change in the environment. A purposeful disposition is really all that's required.

"You don't understand that sometimes there are things you don't need to understand. Understand?"
—Lynn Jackson, Realtor, directional leader spouse, Fellowship Bible Church of Northwest Arkansas

There are times when not needing to know everything is actually a healthy position to embrace.

"Sometimes you have to make a mess so that you can clean a mess up."
—Coleman Peterson, executive vice president for people, Wal-Mart Stores

Placing everything on the table in front of you can be overwhelming, but it may be the only way you can get a clear picture of the direction you should take.

A person with an argument will always be at the mercy of a person with an experience.

—mc

You can talk about perceptions all that you want to, but the reality of anything is the actual experience of it.

Changing your mindset requires constant reinforcement and discipline.

—mc

You change mindsets, not behaviors. Changing mindsets takes a very strong leader, who is willing to challenge his or her own standards of acceptance and entertain the idea that he or she may need to change first before demanding that someone else does.

Are you trying to convince yourself or me?

—mc

Never try to influence others toward a position of acceptance unless you've bought into that position yourself. It's dangerous to your credibility.

"The first responsibility of a leader is to define reality. The last is to say 'thank you.' In between, the leader is a servant."

—Max De Pree, founder, De Pree Leadership Center

Leadership can be defined in many ways. You'd be hard pressed to find a definition as simple and relevant as this.

"Leave no one out of the big picture. Involve everyone in everything of any consequence in all that you do."
—Tom Peters, writer, speaker, consultant

Leaving even one person you depend upon for your success out of the loop can be fatal.

"The best leaders are very often the best listeners. They have an open mind, and they're not interested in having their own way, but in finding the best way."
—Wilfred A. Peterson, author, philosopher

If you surveyed each leader of each company in the *Forbes* 500 and asked them to identify the quality they most admired in either a mentor or a peer, it would be the art of listening.

"There is no exercise better for the heart than reaching down and lifting people up."
—John H. Holmes (1907–1949), minister, Community Church of New York

Still to this day, there is no better reward—emotionally, professionally, or spiritually—than being the catalyst for another's success or salvation.

We used to be the world's moral compass. I think we still are, although in too many instances we're pointing everyone in the wrong direction.
—mc

Too often individuals, institutions, corporations, and even countries compromise their basic beliefs and core values rather than stand in the line of fire for being different and staying true to those beliefs and values.

"The world aches for good listeners. Many doctors report that they see patients daily who have nothing physically wrong with them. They merely need someone to listen to them."
—William E. Diehl, Christian author; president, River Bend Resource Center, Inc.

Listening is an art form chosen by very few as a professional practice, yet it is the one most easily learned, most productive, and most successful, when committed to.

"Laws change, people die, and the land remains."
—Abraham Lincoln, sixteenth president of the United States

Unfortunately, the last time I checked, I think we're affecting that, too.

You know, if you didn't really care, some of these people decisions wouldn't be so tough.
—mc

With few exceptions, people don't get up in the morning with the intent of disrupting another's life by the decisions they make. With really great leaders, caring always gets in the way.

"Be a mentor, not a tormentor."
—Keith Aubele, founder, Acclaim Management

It takes more energy to invest time in the success of others than it does to make their path more difficult to navigate. That's why most people choose the latter activity. The best leaders always choose the first activity and practice it so often and so well that it requires no additional energy because it's character driven.

Live your life in such a way that people look at you and say, "There's something different about that person."

—mc

It takes a high standard of character, moral influence, patience, and empathy to exhibit a lifestyle that other people not only envy, but also want to emulate.

"He who loses money loses much; he who loses a friend loses more; he who loses faith loses it all."
—Eleanor Roosevelt (1884–1962), First Lady of the United States

There are a lot of things in life you can survive without. Friends and faith are not two of them.

"There's a world of difference between being tough and being stupid, and one characteristic is not necessarily exclusive of the other."
—Mark Estes, chiropractor, Bentonville, Arkansas

There's nothing wrong with being perceived as tough and willing to make the hard call. Just be sure you think things through and make your decisions for the right reasons.

"My best friend is the one who brings the best out of me."
—Henry Ford (1863–1947), American auto manufacturer

People meet, beat, or exceed expectations in direct correlation to what they're encouraged to do.

Good people have to have the patience to be rewarded, despite the bad people who get in the way.

     —mc

Educate yourself and learn how to manage difficult people. If you don't, they'll end up managing you right out of a career.

Sometimes life is like an elevator; it goes up and down so fast that it's just better to slow things down by taking the stairs.

     —mc

A sense of urgency is a wonderful character trait to have after the plan has been finalized.

Success can be compared to trying to unlock a door. When you think you're locked out, it might just mean that someone gave you the wrong key.

     —mc

Are you giving your people the wrong keys to the doors you want them to unlock?

"Don't care what others think of what you do, but care very much about what you think you do."
 —St. Francis de Sales (1567–1622), patron saint of authors

The way you think influences what you do. If you care very much about what you do, then others will do the same as a product of your influence.

"When the best leader's work is done, the people say, 'We did it ourselves.'"
  —Lao-tzu, philosopher, father of Taoism, 604 BC

Good ideas come from a lot of different people. In all instances it shouldn't matter who gets the credit as long as the team wins.

"Just when things look their worst, they often change for the best because of the thin line that divides success from failure."
—Ernest Shackleton (1874–1922), Arctic explorer

The second you decide to give up may have been the second that the obstacle to your goal was about to disappear.

"Abraham Lincoln was great, not because he lived in a log cabin, but because he left it."
—Robert Cupp, directional leader, Fellowship Bible Church of Northwest Arkansas

Changing your environment is sometimes the most significant thing you can do to influence your salvation or your success.

"The best leaders have a creative side and look at things differently."
—Robert Lutz, vice chairman, product development, General Motors

The best leaders are always looking for an edge in people, processes, and ideas.

"I could have done something really cool if my boss would have let me."
—Tom Peters, writer, speaker, consultant

Don't let micro-management be one of the character traits you're known for. It's the leadership trait most feared by all subordinates.

"We have to recognize how fast people are capable of going. We're going about as fast as we can now."
—Margaret Wheatley, writer, speaker, consultant

Technology is great, but only if people know how to use it. By nature, people tend to try to do things themselves, which reduces the speed with which you'd like to see things accomplished.

"You must put yourself at risk every day. If people aren't mad at you, you might be dead and not even know it."
—Tom Peters, writer, speaker, consultant

It's impossible to get through any process without upsetting at least one person. It's fine to have conflict as long as it's constructive and beneficial to the end result.

"Diversity means knowing more about your partners."
—Margaret Wheatley, writer, speaker, consultant

True diversity recognizes no boundaries when it comes to race, gender, religion, sex, or otherwise. It's simply the process of knowing all you can about those you happen to come into partnership with, whether by chance, intent, or directive.

There are two kinds of peace: democratic peace, which requires nothing, and dictatorial peace, which requires the consent of silence.
—mc

It's much easier to influence the environment by intimidation and fear than it is by collective collaboration and consensus.

"There is a sufficiency in the world for man's needs but not for man's greed."
—Mahatma Gandhi (1869–1948), Indian philosopher, religious leader

Greed, other than being the simplest to understand, is just one of the many indiscretions influencing corporate leaders today to do things they would not ordinarily do.

"Great minds discuss ideas, average minds discuss events, and small minds discuss people."
—Eleanor Roosevelt (1884–1962), First Lady of the United States

If you don't have anything positive and encouraging to say about someone in public, the best thing to do is to be quiet. Otherwise, share it with them in private and in faith.

"Each time you stand up for an ideal, you send forth a tiny ripple of hope."
—Robert F. Kennedy (1925–1968), U.S. attorney general, senator

Today's world suffers from a severe shortage of dedicated leaders willing to stand up and be heard. The masses will always long desperately for one who understands them, relates to them, and can articulate for them in a way they cannot do for themselves. The risk is great, but the need is greater.

It's a measurable fact that the farther away you are from the top, the more distant the relationship, the less prevalent the recognition, and the smaller the reward.

—mc

It takes one with an unusual amount of concern, passion, and empathy to ensure that everyone is treated fairly, regardless of who or where they are in the pecking order.

"What kind of victory is it when someone is left defeated?"
—Mahatma Gandhi (1869–1948), Indian philosopher, religious leader

In sports, we're taught to win at all costs. In life, we should be taught to help people to win at all ethical costs.

CHAPTER THREE

Politics vs. Integrity

I only know two things for an absolute certainty. There is a God, and in the moment of indecision, always choose integrity.
—Quote by the pastor in the movie *Rudy* (chapel scene)

The author's father and grandmother

My grandmother's name was Mollie Nicks. As I look back, I realize that she was probably one of the most influential people I'll ever know. In a town of three hundred people—Hardy, Arkansas, where I grew up—she was the most recognized person in the community, not because she held a political office or city government position, but because of her personal standing in the community.

She was a member of just about every civic organization that existed and a devout member of the Church of Christ. There wasn't a single individual or family that didn't benefit from her generosity or time during a crisis or illness. As a result, the town named an official week of the year in her honor. I would wager there wasn't anyone in Sharp County that didn't know her personally, wasn't related to her in some way, or at least knew her by name. She also had a sense of urgency that was on display most often when she drove her car. She had both hands on the wheel, eyes fixed straight ahead as if on a mission from above, and the pedal to the floorboard. The thing I remember the most was that her phone rang 24/7 with someone wanting either her time or her advice. It doesn't get much more influential or less political than that.

Phrase	Message
You can't hold dishonest people accountable without honest people stepping forward. —mc	Too often we penalize those in the organization for having a higher standard and choosing to take a stand for basic honesty, rather than stand for even the most minor of dishonest initiatives.
Leadership is serving the agenda, not being the agenda. —mc	When you sacrifice those less practiced, less articulate, less educated, less supported, less politically adept, or simply less accomplished, for the sake of promoting a personal agenda, you should forfeit any claim to honest leadership.

"People just want a single version of the truth."
—Tom Coughlin, executive vice chairman, board of directors, Wal-Mart Stores

Rather than spend so much time trying to determine how to script information so that it will have the least negative outcome, spend your time scripting it for the maximum positive outcome. There is a difference.

"Politics is the art of looking for trouble, finding it everywhere, diagnosing it incorrectly, and applying the wrong remedies."
—Groucho Marx (1890–1977), comedian

Those who spend all their time trying to influence everyone around them for no apparent reason always have an agenda. They never talk about it, but all too often they realize their goal at the expense of others.

"There is no such thing as a minor lapse of integrity."
—Tom Peters, writer, speaker, consultant

Thinking that a minor lapse is insignificant is the ultimate in rationalization.

People leave the leader, not the organization.
—mc

Turnover in corporate America is at an all-time high. Survey after survey still indicates that the number-one reason for turnover is less because of the organization than because of the lack of consistency by the leader in charge of the organization.

There are two types of managers: those who do the work and those who take the credit. Try to be in the first group. There's a lot less competition.

—mc

Accomplishing goals only through political connections may produce desired results, even for extended periods of time. What it will produce for certain in a very short period of time is a lack of respect, a lack of trust, and a lack of credibility that will last forever.

Because they're reclusive, some people are accused of living in their own little world. I think maybe it's just because they know everyone who lives there.

—mc

Relationships require the largest investment of time we have, regardless of what we do. It's just a little easier if you happen to be relational by nature.

If you're going to depend upon others for your success, then the words "thank you" need to become a lot more important than the word "please."

—mc

Dependence upon people can be a very tricky enterprise based entirely upon whether or not you have an agenda. What goes around always, without exception, comes back around.

Be humble. A lot was accomplished before you were born.

—mc

Humility is not an indication of weakness and is a very good trait for a leader to have. To respect those who've come before you, those who are currently around you, and especially those who are new to join you, inspires people to trust.

Artificial enthusiasm is dangerous. Sometimes it's not how you respond but what you've learned.

—mc

It's great to want to please others unless you fail to pick up enough through the experience to actually add value. If you don't, you become expendable.

"An appeaser is one who feeds a crocodile, hoping it will eat him last."
—Winston Churchill (1874–1965), English prime minister

When all your activities have only the purpose of survival rather than contribution and value, then your future over the long term can be predicted with a great degree of accuracy.

"It's people, people, always people."
—Andy Wilson, CEO, Soderquist Center for Leadership and Ethics

People accomplish only through other people. This will never change.

"I can predict your future with a fair degree of accuracy by talking to just a few of your people."
—Sam Walton (1918–1992), founder, Wal-Mart Stores

If you haven't gotten it by now, it's people, always people.

I've got a problem going to war for anyone who takes casualties too lightly.

—mc

When leaders show a lack of respect, concern, and empathy for those under their supervision, especially when loss of employment or family occurs, the leader should have no expectation of support, loyalty, or trust.

"Why forfeit three fourths of yourself just to be like other people?"
—Arthur Schopenhauer (1788–1860), philosopher

If you're not careful, you can spend your entire career trying to win someone else's approval, when all you really needed was your own.

If everyone thinks like you do, why do you keep asking for information?

—mc

Don't keep asking people for feedback if you're not going to take them seriously. To do so may to you be politically correct, but to those you're asking, a very insincere effort to give the perception that you care.

If your primary goal is to make sure that everyone likes and approves of you, then you risk sacrificing your uniqueness and, therefore, your excellence.

—mc

Having approval as a primary goal most often places people where they didn't want to be in the first place—on the outside looking in.

You might be wrong when you say that someone is not a team player. You just might not understand that it's their team.

—mc

If you line up behind someone who professes to be a leader, be careful. They may be running for office rather than actually leading.

"Be sure and measure the credibility factor when evaluating whether someone who professes to be a leader actually is a leader."
—Lou Tice, founder, The Pacific Institute

You should ask three questions: Why should I listen to you; in other words, how are you like me? Have you ever managed or coached someone like me to success? Do you know what you're talking about; in other words, do you have real life experience?

"Always do right. This will gratify most people and astonish the rest. "
—Mark Twain (1835–1910), humorist, author

This has never been truer at any time in our country's history than today, where we live in a corporate culture that has allowed a tolerance of dishonesty that defies description.

"Integrity is what we do, what we say, and what we say we do."
—Don Galer, author

I almost expected to find this definition beside the word "integrity" in the dictionary. It's never been said any better.

"The only sacred cow in an organization is its principles."
—Buck Rodgers, professional baseball manager

Principles are what you stand for and what you are. They're not to be modified or violated, or the whole organization is at risk.

"Fidelity means do not change the identity of the lesson and its intent."
—Dr. Archie Hensley, Africa Inland Missions

When you decide to change the commitment in a message you've already delivered, that's the moment you begin to lose credibility.

It's always better to be a prospect than suspect.
—mc

Monitor everything you do in such a way that you're never suspected of anything but good motives.

"Your target group is not interested in answers to questions they're not asking."
—Dr. Archie Hensley, Africa Inland Missions

The longer you talk without dealing with the subject matter at hand, the sooner you lose credibility with your target group.

When substance matches image, then you've got the real deal.
—mc

This is why true leaders are so rare. The ability to live life as you portray it is truly a matter of moral discipline.

Are you talking to your people or just running for office?
—mc

People know the difference. Don't make the mistake of thinking they don't. People put you where they want you based upon how they feel about you, which can sometimes be where you don't want to be.

30

"When people respect you, they forgive you. When they fear you, they think only about survival, not forgiveness."
—Andy Wilson, CEO, Soderquist Center for Leadership/Ethics

Survey after survey has proven that a leadership style based upon fear and intimidation has about a two- to five-year life span, depending upon the size of the organization.

"Human action can be modified to some extent, but human nature cannot be changed."
—Abraham Lincoln, sixteenth president of the United States

Most people are political to some degree—if not by nature, at least by circumstance. It's when someone is political by nature regardless of the circumstance that everyone suffers.

"If, as a corporate manager, you cannot support your employee's position, be sure you at least support the employee."
—Roger Herman, consultant, speaker, futurist

One of the best ways of ensuring that people don't leave your organization is to support them as individuals, especially at times when it may not be popular to do so.

"Whether we inherit power, attain it gradually, or receive it by virtue of being elected to a specific post, it doesn't really belong to us and we have no guarantee that it will last. The only thing we know for sure is that, for as long as we have it, we're responsible for using it wisely."
—Stephen Graves, Thomas Addington, cofounders, The Life@Work Co.

Our responsibility is to use everything in our power for the common good and not for personal gain.

CHAPTER FOUR

Humor—The Great Sustainer!

*Two Quaker women in a railway coach in 1861
overheard as follows:*

"I think Jefferson will succeed," said the first.
"Why doest thee think so?" asked the second.
"Because Jefferson is a praying man," said the first.
"And so is Lincoln a praying man," said the second.
"Yes, but the Lord will think Lincoln is joking."

—Abraham Lincoln, sixteenth president
of the United States

The author

I can't imagine what I must have been thinking. I'll give you
some comical visual detail by telling you that what you're seeing is
a bright rust–colored, two-piece leisure suit; a flowered, polyester

casual shirt with the tail out and open midway to the chest; a pair of black, wool dress socks; and a pair of mahogany, three-inch, platform shoes. This was taken right before attending a Christmas dance with a young lady I was trying to impress. How impressed do you think she was when during the dance, as I was busting what I thought was one of my best moves, the heels popped off those shoes and I fell flat on my rear end? It wasn't one of my more defining moments, but certainly one of the more humorous. As my dad would have said, I looked like the cat's meow.

Phrase

We don't throw people out. We aggressively place them elsewhere.

—mc

Message

This is a description that might apply to downsizing initiatives taken by several major corporations.

"Here's the deal. You've got an opinion, and I've got an opinion. Let me just say that in this instance, the only difference is that mine counts."

—Ed Hudnall, regional vice president, Wal-Mart Stores

Good advice given to a manager while discussing why a directive wasn't being followed as given. We should all understand that for the common good, some directions aren't optional.

"Son, I believe you've about peaked here."

—Robert L. (Big Bob) Hart, vice president, Wal-Mart Stores

This was a response to an individual who just wouldn't accept the fact that, appropriately so, he wasn't going to be promoted at that particular time.

"Be cheerful! Of all the things you wear, your expression is the most important."
—Ralph Waldo Emerson (1803–1882), American author, poet

Studies have proven that, over time, those individuals who are the most successful are those who have a willingness to take risks, a continuous desire for improvement, a low resistance to change, and a generally positive, cheerful personality.

There are parts of me so private that even I myself have no knowledge of them.

—mc

Having levity enough to laugh at oneself is a valuable commodity.

It's not a given that the organization will respond to you just because you've been there since the earth cooled.

—mc

Advice given during a moment of levity to help a manager who'd been employed for a number of years understand why he'd been passed over for promotion.

Sometimes you have to use the Barney Fife method of management and just "nip it, nip it, nip it."

—mc

This was an example given to encourage a manager who was known for procrastinating with difficult decisions.

"It's not a termination offense to be less or more intelligent than your supervisor."
—H. Lee Scott, president, CEO, Wal-Mart Stores

How insecure do you have to be to disregard the value of a member of your team to the point of sacrificing them to turnover?

"The only thing I can say is that at the end of the day, someone's going to be missing."
—Ed Hudnall, senior vice president, Wal-Mart Stores

This was an appropriate fact pointed out during an internal loss prevention audit regarding stolen store funds.

"When I drive I never get lost. I just change where I'm going."
—Rita Rudner, comedian

What a great attitude to have at times when dealing with uncertainty.

"You can't give a hummingbird a drink with a fire hose."
—Dr. Archie Hensley, Africa Inland Missions

There's great danger in giving people too much information to process at one time.

Whatever it is that you just explained to me, Fred and Ginger couldn't have done it any better.
—mc

There are many explanations given in response to accountability that are inadequate, political, and bureaucratic. Stop dancing and just tell the truth.

Stick a fork in it. I think it's done.

           —unknown

This was an observation made indicating that the subject had been discussed more than necessary.

If more than twenty people tell you you're dead, you might want to consider lying down.

           —mc

This was an observation made to a manager who didn't want to accept responsibility for an improper decision after several peers and subordinates had indicated otherwise.

"The reason some people get lost in thought is because it's unfamiliar territory."

           —Charles F. Kettering
           (1876–1958), author

Having the ability and discipline to plan your business is one of the best ways to ensure your success.

Are you one of those who believe Humpty Dumpty was pushed?

           —mc

This was an observation made to a manager to illustrate the presence of a negative disposition in that individual's leadership style.

"That statement barely borders on being brilliant."
—Nancy Wetmore, manager of policy and communications for logistics, Wal-Mart Stores, Inc.

This was an observation made to an overbearing people manager during a human resource discussion regarding the development of corporate employee benefits.

"Business is about common sense, which is not all that common."
—Robert A. Lutz, vice chairman, product development, General Motors

This was an observation made while speaking to a consortium of human resource managers regarding the subject of placing too much emphasis upon recruiting the degree instead of the person.

I really like you and I'm hoping that we can come to some kind of understanding, because if we don't, we may have to free up your future.
—mc

There are times when there is no amount of influence that will motivate a person to change when that change is critical to the organization and critical to that person's future. Then you have to spell it out.

I don't know how we're going to do without you, but starting tomorrow we may have to find out.
—mc

There are times when you can take only so much from someone who thinks and acts as if they're entirely indispensable.

"Sometimes you need to be rigidly flexible."
—Mary Cohagen, administrative assistant (retired), Wal-Mart Stores

There are times to bend, and there are times to stand firm, but there is never a time to break.

"People who never get carried away should be."
—Malcolm Forbes, American publisher

People who never display enthusiasm, energy, and a sense of urgency can stifle the growth of an organization as severely as any other negative element.

By some people's definition, people who always agree with them have a very bright future.
—mc

Great leaders remind those under their supervision on a regular basis that challenge is healthy, necessary for the organization, and welcomed positively when offered.

Problems usually come in four sizes; small, medium, large, and "Get the elephant gun, Ethel. I think I see one coming."
—mc

Most problems that appear too large to manage at first seem to shrink in enormity after the time has been taken to really think them through.

If you're expecting me to have an out-of-body experience based upon what you've just told me, I may not meet your expectations.
—mc

There is value in controlling your response to the degree that it doesn't overly alarm those who look to you for that kind of control.

Don't let your mouth write a check your rear end can't cover.
—mc

There are times when the best substitute for intelligence is silence.

"The difference between 'think and do jobs' and 'think and delegate jobs' depends on whether it's just you or not."
—Glen Shank, president/CEO, Duckwall-ALCO Stores, Inc.

Know who, when, how, where, and what when it comes to managing your resources.

Why would you want to walk in someone else's shoes, especially if they don't fit?
—mc

There is only one you, and that is your legacy, whether you like it or not. So embrace it with enthusiasm and hope.

When it's all said and done, we may not all end up holding hands and singing the Coke song together, but maybe we can at least start tuning up.
—mc

There rarely has to be an end-all, be-all decision, when a possible compromise is the most effective solution at the time.

You've heard it said that you can lead a horse to water, but you can't make it drink. What do you figure the odds are if it hasn't had a drink all day?
—mc

Never assume you know everything you think you do about your point of focus. More history has been made as a result of the unknown than of the known.

40

I'm not totally sure, but I think your rear end just left the room.

—mc

It's wise to know when you've made your position clear. To go beyond that point can, at times, be somewhat unhealthy for a career.

You're backpedaling faster than a crawfish in a creek bank.

—mc

Be sure you're willing to stand for what you say. There's nothing worse for your credibility than reversing your position in a manner perceived as the politically correct thing to do.

You appear to have a "hitch" in your "get-a-long."

—mc

Do your homework. Your credibility is influenced by how well you prepare.

We're going to do something to you, but we just don't know what it is yet.

—mc

There's a heavy price to pay for short-term management thinking when retaining or separating people from your organization without having thought it through.

"I'm sorry. They don't tell me anything. I just work here."

—An employee to my wife while shopping in an arts and crafts store

This is the feeling I get from too many employees in too many workplaces where it appears that information beneficial to their success with the organization is not being freely and openly shared with them.

The food here is lousy, and the portions are so small.
—unknown

Human nature at times dictates such a focus on the negatives, regardless of how significant, are not just overlooked, but buried.

"No one is worthless. They may be a bad example, but never worthless."
—H. Lee Scott, president, CEO, Wal-Mart Stores

There should be an awful lot of energy expended to save people before arriving at a decision to separate them from the organization. They're too difficult to replace.

Unless you can impress someone with that spotted-owl trick, you might want to look at people when they're talking to you.
—mc

The art of communication requires eye contact, which inspires honesty, directness, and trustworthiness.

I never thought of that because it's suicide.
—mc

There are things said that at times, along with requiring no consideration, are so obvious they reveal the ignorance of the speaker.

"Blessed is he who has learned to laugh at himself, for he shall never cease to be entertained."
—John Powell, motivational author

Recent studies have shown that of all of the character traits men possess, a sense of humor is the one valued most by the majority.

Instructions for speaking before thinking: Open mouth, insert foot, and chew vigorously.

—mc

It's amazing how those who speak in a politically correct manner for personal gain do so with such enthusiasm and lack of respect for the intelligence of those to whom they speak.

There's no trailer hitch on a hearse.

—unknown

Think seriously about what you leave behind, not only on a daily basis, but in the course of a lifetime. The memory of what you are will live long after any material possessions you may be hanging onto.

I had the best times in my life there, especially after I left.

—mc

There are times when hanging on to something you think you want more than anything in the world can be so damaging. I think it's true that letting go of something is the only way of finding out if it was meant to be yours.

"You love your brothers and sisters, but you're going to get to the table first, aren't you?"
—Tom Coughlin, executive vice chairman, board of directors, Wal-Mart Stores

Even members of your own family may become your competitors, depending upon what everyone is competing for.

"If your feet moved as fast as your mouth, you'd be a superstar."

—Nike

The easiest activity for a person to participate in is talking. The hardest, but most productive by far, is listening.

One way to get high blood pressure is to go mountain climbing over molehills.

—unknown

A great character trait for a leader to have is the ability to calmly and objectively process negative information in a way that will instill confidence and trust rather than panic and chaos.

Sometimes you have to practice the "YOOH" program. That means "You're out of here!"

—mc

Every organization should have a narrow set of principles that, if violated, simply allow no discussion for latitude. There should be a philosophical, moral culture that insists that those who do not agree do not belong.

"The biggest things to do are often the easiest to do because there is so little competition."

—William Van Horne (1843–1915), general manager, Canadian Pacific Railway

The harder the task, the fewer people there are willing to undertake it. It's the essence of human nature and the one weakness great leaders always exploit.

"All truth passes through three stages. First, it's ridiculed. Second, it's violently opposed. Third, it's accepted as being self-evident."
—Arthur Schopenhauer (1788–1860), German philosopher

How long can you rationalize the truth before you're willing to take responsibility for it?

When I'm asked why someone was able to accomplish something they were never perceived as being capable of, my response is that they must not have known any better.

—mc

In today's world, great accomplishments are becoming the norm for individuals who are younger in age, maturity, and wisdom than at any point in our country's history. It's because their thought process is not limited by historical thinking, parameters, or obstacles that might prevent the discovery of new ways of doing things.

Have you noticed how some people don't think they're sick until they go see the doctor?

—mc

We may know more about ourselves as individuals than anyone alive, yet we're often willing to let certified strangers convince us we're under the influence of something that's out of our control, especially if it happens to conveniently coincide with some external pressure we'd rather avoid.

There is a world of difference in the mindset of one who sits motionless in a barn full of manure for fear of getting soiled compared to the one who looks without ceasing in hopes of finding the pony that should, by all calculations, be there somewhere.
> —Based on an old concept of unknown origin about the difference between optimists and pessimists

Regardless of the severity of dire circumstances, looking for the opportunity to change them is the only alternative.

"Well-behaved women rarely make history."
> —Laurel Thatcher Ulrich, author, professor of Early American history

The glass ceiling is not influenced by depending upon others to modify the playing field. It's influenced by creating an environment that will allow you to accomplish what you feel is your right to have.

"There are three things that are real: God, human folly, and laughter. The first two are beyond our comprehension, so we must do what we can with the third."
> —John F. Kennedy, thirty-fifth president of the United States

Sometimes explanations are unavailable. You must choose to believe based upon faith, respond based upon concern, or laugh out loud with relief.

When making your reservations for eternity, please indicate whether you prefer smoking or nonsmoking.
—Taken from a road sign in front of a church somewhere in Mississippi

I'm convinced that it would really be beneficial to know the difference.

Everyone doing what one person says is some folks' definition of teamwork.
—unknown

There is a fine line between directing and delegating.

The only reason people say that no one lives forever is that no one has ever done it.
—mc

No human ever will! Some people just need to realize it and live life accordingly.

Oops! My fault! I was born with a personality.
—mc

If you don't recognize that each individual under your umbrella of responsibility is just that, an individual, then your desire to manage everyone the same way will soon be adjusted for you.

"It's not that I don't like change. I just don't like to be there when it happens."
—Comment by the obsessive-compulsive detective on the television show *Monk*

For the most part people, by nature, don't like change. Adapting to change is so much easier if time is taken on the front end to sell the change first.

I learned a while ago that if no one can read your writing, you don't have to be concerned too much about shredding your paperwork.

—mc

Never do, say, or write something you wouldn't want anyone you're leading to do, hear, or read.

Privatization vs. regulation keeps the masses from being unfairly penalized.

—mc

Most rules and regulations are created for the masses as a result of the behavior of a very few. By nature, it's easier to use the shotgun than the rifle.

Are we going to really discuss this or just "ankle peck" it to death?

—mc

This was an observation made to the facilitator of a meeting where one particular subject of minor importance had been danced around for the better part of two hours.

"Sometimes you have to tell people what they think they know."
—Sam Dunn, CFO, Sam's Club, Wal-Mart Stores

There are times when you have to validate instincts rather than waiting until the reporting deadline. No one likes surprises, especially when you're reporting earnings.

"Is this the hill you really want to die on?"
—Ed Nagy, senior vice president, Wal-Mart Stores

Think long and hard about whether you really feel it's worth it to pursue a subject when feelings have been made quite clear.

Some mice need to be milked.

       —mc

There are some minor issues that need to be resolved. Just don't misdiagnose the importance or the size of the issue.

There are only two ways to lose money: either real slow or real fast.

       —mc

A total focus on the bottom line will not alleviate a minor or major profit loss, especially if factors influencing that loss are not a part of the focus.

A day without some humor is a wasted day.

       —unknown

I can't imagine, nor do I ever hope to discover, what an entire day would be like without at least one inner, humorous thought that might elicit at least a second of lightheartedness.

My experience is that all the communication takes place before lunch and all the processing takes place after lunch. The opportunity is that most of the resources you need for the processing are in and out in the afternoon.

       —mc

This may seem humorous, and is to some degree, but it's as accurate a description as I can come up with as to what's wrong in today's workplace, regardless of the profession.

"If you're going to hire someone from outside your company who's incompetent, why don't you look inside your company first?"
—H. Lee Scott, president, CEO, Wal-Mart Stores

It's advisable and often appropriate to bring someone in from outside your organization for the purpose of tapping into fresh ideas, new perspectives, and exceptional talent. But to do so very often at the expense of talent that already exists inside your organization can be unhealthy in the long term.

CHAPTER FIVE

Spiritual Influence

It's been said that the devil is in the details, and it's also been said that God is in the details. So until you get into the details, you may not know who you're dealing with.

—Maxie Carpenter

The author and his mother

My mother is and always has been a spiritual person. She made sure we were in church every Sunday morning, Sunday evening, and Wednesday evening. Sunday school was conducted for both adults and children one hour before the worship service started. The entire congregation numbered about a hundred altogether, when everyone attended. There was no child care service, no kids' church, no singles ministry, no counseling ministry, no community outreach program, no missions initiative, no men's or women's ministry, and so on. Everyone just took care of everyone else as the need arose. Sunday afternoons were usually given to either visiting the surrounding nursing homes or the hospital with Grandma Mollie or attending a young people's meeting at the church. We always had a potluck dinner after church at Grandma's house, our house, or the house of a member of the congregation. It was just tradition. I think I still have a few permanent pop-knots on my head from those knuckle thumpers I used to get when I wouldn't sit still. Between Mom and Grandma, they could reach me no matter where I sat on that pew. Looking back, I wouldn't have wished for it any other way.

Phrase

"Are you ambitious for the right things?"
—Robert Cupp, founder, Fellowship Bible Church of Northwest Arkansas

People pray in their time. God answers prayer in his own.
—unknown

Message

Are your motives pure and influenced by morality and honesty? Ambition is a great character trait to have if it's focused on the right things and based upon a pure and unadulterated consideration and respect for those around you.

It's fine to wish and pray for all that we'd like to have. How urgently, sincerely, unselfishly, respectfully, and humbly we work for what we'd like to have through those around us is a true indicator of how quickly and positively we'll be rewarded.

"I do not feel obliged to believe that the same God, who has endowed us with sense, reason, and intellect, has intended us to forgo their use."
  —Galileo (1564–1642), astronomer and physicist

Do not waste or foolishly use the talents and abilities the good Lord has blessed you with. To do so is such a grave indiscretion.

"Surely God would not have created such a being as man, with an ability to grasp the infinite, to exist for only one day. No, no, man, through God, was made for immortality."
  —Abraham Lincoln, sixteenth president of the United States

In spite of all the scientific logic used over the course of history to explain the existence of mankind, it's just simply too awesome to have happened by accident.

If Methuselah were standing here today, he would tell you that life is too short.
  —mc

Life is so short, especially as you get older. Don't waste time on unworthy endeavors. Focus only on those that are honorable and worthy of your time and energy.

Service is rent paid for life on earth.
  —unknown

To serve others continuously is an honorable and worthy accomplishment.

You get to talk to God every day. It doesn't get much better than that.

—mc

There's a lot of comfort in knowing that you don't need an appointment, you don't need to call ahead, you don't need a special pass, you don't have to have a special position, you don't have to know anyone important, you don't need transportation, you don't need any money to get in, and you don't need anyone with you. He's the easiest ticket in town.

There are politics, even in heaven. You can't get in unless you know the Son!

—mc

It will always be true that knowing someone important and having a relationship with him or her gives you an edge that most of those people around you don't have.

"The integrity of the message is equal to the integrity of the messenger."
—Dr. Archie Hensley,
Africa Inland Missions

What is said is not always a reflection of what is thought, although, without exception, it should be.

A guru is one who is a teacher and especially intellectual guide in matters of funda- mental concern; one who is an acknowledged leader or chief proponent.
—Merriam-Webster's Online

Based upon the importance of this definition, be careful to whom you entrust your development, training, mentoring, and character building.

I'm going to quit coming to church if I'm the only one he's going to keep talking to.
—unknown

How many times do you have to hear the same message, whether positive, constructive, negative, or otherwise, before you begin to believe it?

You don't change behav- iors. You change mindsets.
—mc

The way people behave is directed by the way they think. The way they think is a matter of character. The character is the mindset. Only the person is in charge of the mindset, and only the person can change it.

"When it's dark enough, you can see the stars."
—Ralph Waldo Emerson (1803–1882), author, poet

Sometimes you have to get so far down to the bottom before you realize that it's only a place to turn around. Then you have no choice but to look up.

Be careful that you don't become so open-minded that your brain falls out.
—mc

Stay true to your values, your tolerance levels, your faith, your family, and your basic beliefs. They are the true guides to success and happiness.

"Never compromise your-self. You're all you've got."
—Betty Ford,
First Lady of the United States

There will never be another you. Make your legacy count.

"When people go to work, they shouldn't have to leave their hearts at home."
—Betty Bender, author,
organizational consultant

Leaders sometimes create an environment that doesn't al-low employees to be true to themselves and their basic beliefs. If the culture doesn't support common beliefs, values, and goals, people will leave.

"God will not look you over for medals, degrees, or diplomas. He'll look for scars."
—Elbert Hubbard (1856–
1915), editor, author,
founder, Roycrofters

Do what always matters, not what always rewards.

The one statistic that is not an estimate is that one out of one dies.
—mc

Don't make the mistake of thinking that you can exist without considering eternity. Personally, I wouldn't want to be eternally surprised in the end.

"Truth discovered has a much greater impact than truth imposed."
—Dr. Archie Hensley, Africa Inland Missions

Deception only delays the inevitable. The truth will be known, and it won't be your truth that's important, but how it's perceived.

"People need your love the most when they appear to deserve it the least."
—John Harrigan, rock music promoter, Sydney, Australia, 1960

The hardest thing for leaders to do is to spend time with the people they like the least.

If the impossible is not in my plans, then God is not one of my partners.
—mc

Only a fool would be willing to take the chance that there isn't a God and that there isn't an eternity of some kind in store for them.

"Leading others to Christ is more a process of removing the obstacles that are preventing others from seeing Christ so that they can see him for themselves."
—Chip Jackson, Saturday Night directional leader, Fellowship Bible Church of Northwest Arkansas

One of our human flaws is, at times, to give ourselves too much credit for doing things when, in reality, we were simply the conduit through which things happened.

"It's strange that we all defend our wrongs with more vigor than we do our rights."
—Kahlil Gibran (1883–1931), Lebanese-born American author and poet

This statement could be made about a wide segment of corporate leaders today, who are given so many resources, money, and power, and yet are held to so little accountability for abusing so many people. That's just pure insanity.

"I still say a church steeple with a lightning rod on top shows a lack of confidence."
—Doug McLeod, author

There are those extremists, even in the church, who dare God on a regular basis to prove them wrong. They'd do well to remember that he always gets around to giving everyone what they really deserve.

CHAPTER SIX

Saving People vs. Replacing Them

There is no nobler act than saving someone's career.
—Leroy Schuetts, senior vice president, Wal-Mart Stores

Mr. Sam and the author (1985)

At the age of sixteen, I was what was commonly referred to as a gym rat. I would stay after school every day by myself to practice some part of my game. On one of these days I had my first meeting with Sam Walton. He came in the gym wearing a sweatsuit and started running laps to warm up. When he was finished, he asked me if I wanted to play some. I said sure, so we played until it was time for me to go home. As I was gathering my things, he asked me what I wanted to do when I got out of school. I told him I didn't have a clue. He told me that if I ever needed a job, to let him know. Seven years later, I was looking for a part-time job while going to college. I stopped in at the Wal-Mart in Rogers, Arkansas, and put in an application. Remembering what he'd told me a few years before, I put his name down as the only reference I had. When I was hired in September 1973, I was told that they'd called Mr. Sam to see if I actually knew him. He remembered me and told them to hire me, saying that "he would be a good one." That defining event influenced me to model a philosophy that respects everyone, regardless of stature, and helps as many people as possible to win.

Phrase	Message
Most companies spend more time on the back end getting rid of people than they do on the front end selecting good people. —mc	We're all familiar with Robert Deming's "Total Quality" philosophy of doing it right the first time. It's never more applicable than in the process of choosing the right person for the right position.
As long as managers mismanage, there is job security for anyone who works in human resources. —mc	It should become a goal of any manager to care for their people so that lawyers, labor relations managers, arbitration supervisors, and other similar human resource specialists become unnecessary.
No one is born with the natural ability to do anything that is not biologically inherited. They have to be taught. —mc	Training is the number-two reason (behind poor leadership) that people leave their current work environment.

"A diamond is a chunk of coal that made good under pressure."

—unknown

You never know how good someone can really be until you give them a chance to prove it. Even your best assumptions might be challenged if you're willing to take the risk.

If you could save one person by just listening, wouldn't you have to do that?

—mc

Listening is the number-one activity that people want from the person they report to.

As a mentor, if you're someone's door of opportunity, how often are you home?

—mc

It's a tremendous obligation and responsibility to commit to the success of an individual who's chosen you as a role model and mentor. If you accept that challenge, don't accept it lightly. You have to own that contribution.

Most small engines operate efficiently on two parts gasoline and one part oil. Likewise, most people respond to two parts discipline and one part recognition.

—mc

People, much like small engines, won't respond to the appropriate degree without either one.

There's no such thing as a lazy person. They're either sick or uninspired.

—mc

The most difficult thing to do when trying to motivate someone you're struggling with is to take a look at yourself first and ask whether or not you're holding up your end of the relationship.

If you say you will take care of it, then do it.

—mc

Most managers don't realize that this is the simplest form of commitment, yet the one most often violated. Failure to take care of your responsibilities undermines relationships daily.

"Expect people to be better than they are; it helps them to become better. But don't be disappointed when they're not; it helps them to keep trying."
—Merry Browne, author

The greatest motivation for people who really care about getting better is not knowing they'll suffer some sort of discipline, but knowing that you'll be disappointed in them, yet still care about them.

Never underestimate the value of a good person.

—mc

There are people in any organization who may not be as proficient, intelligent, progressive, or contemporary as those on the fast track, but they shouldn't be overlooked. They can still bring moral value to the table.

We could probably recruit more new Christians if we could keep folks away from the old ones.

—mc

The hypocrisy in most organizations exists in the ranks of those who've been around for a long time and profess to support the culture. They won't lift a hand to save those who've recently joined the ranks and are struggling as a result of challenging the way things have always been done.

"Many times, people are lost because the people at the top don't have the talent to recognize the talent in the people at the bottom."
—Mike Merrill, senior partner, Diversified Retail Solutions

It doesn't matter how much "executive" talent you have. If you don't have the ability to recognize talent in others, you don't have the ability to help your organization survive.

The only ones who didn't commit any turnovers were the ones who didn't get to play.

—mc

More great people are lost to organizations every day because they didn't get an opportunity to contribute.

If you can't teach someone, don't criticize them. The ability to teach has nothing to do with age and everything to do with attitude.

—mc

The easiest way to get rid of someone who's not meeting expectations is to criticize them rather than doing the most difficult thing, which is to teach them. Interestingly enough, most supervisors will not teach because they're not capable of doing so. I've always wondered how that worked to anyone's benefit.

"If you have to build a case, you don't have one."
—Becky Wilson, wife of Andy Wilson, CEO, Soderquist Center for Leadership and Ethics

Rather than trying so hard to get rid of people, why don't you work just as hard to save them?

Your success will be determined far more by those who work for you than by those you work for.

—mc

This is and will continue to be the one truism relevant to managing people in any organization, whether it be a home, a church, a company, or otherwise.

"To be an effective teacher, every leader should have the willingness, not the need, to be admired."
—Lou Tice, founder, The Pacific Institute

A teacher must be willing to accept the fact that being admired goes along with the territory because that's what people do when someone helps them succeed.

"Could a greater miracle take place than for us to look through each other's eyes for an instant?"
—Henry David Thoreau (1817–1862), author, essayist, philosopher

One of the most difficult things for a leader to do is to empathize, which means to try to imagine how the other person must feel.

"In heroic organizations, people mentor each other unselfishly."
—Dan Zadra, strategic planning consultant, author

Mentoring is the ultimate in displaying how much you care about someone else's success.

"Next to doing a good job yourself, the greatest joy is in helping someone else do a first-class job under your direction."
—William Feather (1908–1976), author, publisher

I know of few greater joys than knowing you are directly responsible for another's success.

People, by nature, do exactly what you tell them to do and, by nature, believe exactly what you tell them to believe.
—mc

This is commonly referred to as a self-fulfilling prophecy. More people fail because of this shortsighted leadership approach than any I know of.

People, for the most part, remain the same from the day they're born until the day they die. They are only changed by the way other people treat them.

—mc

We are all products of our experiences, beginning with those who conceived us.

"A ship in harbor is safe, but that is not what ships are built for."
—John A. Shedd, author

More people fail because they're not encouraged. People, for the most part, have to be pushed out of their comfort zone so that they can realize their gift or their greatness.

CHAPTER SEVEN

Accountability

We have to be able to count on each other doing what we have agreed to do.

—Phil Crosby, international quality
management consultant

The author and his father talking things over

I can't remember my dad ever laying a hand on me. I don't think it was because he didn't believe in sparing the rod as much as it was because he relied more upon the power of emotional influence. He had a way of making you feel worse because you felt that you'd disappointed him than the expectation of the pain that any whipping could inflict. I can actually remember times when I wished that he'd just get after me with the belt rather than talk to me. I always knew when it was time to "melt things down," as he would say. He'd come in after work and say, "Son, let's go for a ride." A "ride" meant anywhere from thirty minutes to an hour (depending on the seriousness of the issue) around town or in the surrounding rural area. I think that's another reason that, to this day, rather than "airing out the laundry," I refuse to have a confrontation with anyone in front of others.

It shouldn't be a surprise then to know that I practice the same philosophy as my father did about holding people accountable. And if you were to talk to my son, he'd tell you that he dreads those rides worse than anything.

⟨◎⟩→

Phrase

Message

"Argue for your limitations and, sure enough, they're yours."
—Richard Bach, author, philosopher, descendant of Johann Sebastian Bach

It's been proven over and over that if you say something enough times, you eventually come to believe it. Defending yourself on the basis of limitations in the face of accountability can be very risky.

"Aerodynamically the bumblebee shouldn't be able to fly, but because it doesn't know that, it goes on flying anyway."
—Mary Kay Ash (1915–2001), founder, Mary Kay Cosmetics

Great things can be accomplished by simply knowing there are no limitations on what you're able to do in order to accomplish a given task.

"Most people never run far enough on their first wind to find out if they've got a second one."
—William James (1842–1910), psychologist, philosopher

How do you know what you're capable of if you don't push yourself harder than anyone else would?

"It's easy to dodge our responsibilities, but we cannot dodge the consequences of dodging our responsibilities."
—Sir Josiah Stamp (1880–1941), director, Bank of England

Those who become complacent with their responsibilities lack one quality that most great leaders have in common, and that's the ability to look ahead and visualize inevitable outcomes.

"When you get right down to the root meaning of the word 'succeed,' you'll find it simply means to follow through."
—F. W. Nichol, author, motivational consultant

The character trait most appreciated by supervisors of those reporting to them is the ability to follow through to successful completion.

"Keep changing. When you're through changing, you're through."
—Bruce Barton (1886–1967), author; congressman; founder, BBDO ad agency; creator of Betty Crocker

The speed of change in today's business environment is almost as fast as the speed of sound. If you can't change at that rate, your chances of success are very limited.

"When one door closes, another opens, but we often look so long and regretfully at the closed one that we don't see the one that was opened for us."
—Alexander Graham Bell (1847–1922), Scottish inventor (telephone)

Getting out of your comfort zone is an absolute requirement in today's business world. When companies downsize, the first to go are those who resist change.

"It's not only what we do, but also what we do not do, for which we are accountable."
—Molière (1622–1673), French playwright

This is as true with what we say as it is with what we do. More great tragedies have been wrought by what was omitted than by what was actually said.

"The moment you commit and quit holding back, all sorts of unforeseen incidents, meetings, and material assistance will rise up to help you. The simple act of commitment is a powerful magnet for help."
—Napoleon Hill, motivational author

There's nothing better for success than a single-minded focus.

"Take risks. You can't fall off the bottom."
—Barbara Proctor, author and communicator

Sometimes the best attitude to have is that you have nothing to lose and everything to gain by giving it your best, committed shot.

"When you give up accountability, you become unnecessary."
— Lou Tice, founder, The Pacific Institute

No one should hold you more accountable than you do yourself.

We design accountability measures for the masses, based on the behavior of a few.
— mc

Focus on people who aren't being accountable rather than on those who are.

"Some athletes believe more in someone else's game than they do their own."
— Davis Love III, professional golfer

If you spend more time admiring someone else's progress than you do focusing on your own, you can easily become expendable.

If you don't believe, then let someone else who does take your place.
— mc

There's little to be gained by doing something you've no interest in.

My daughter is only thirteen years old. What's your excuse?
— mc

The only victims I know are children and those in elder care. Don't become a victim. It's the quickest path to unemployment.

On extremely rare occasions, the best plan is actually no plan. Just do something!
— mc

There are times when waiting on the plan is not an appropriate response to a dire emergency.

You have to get there first before you can stay there.
—mc

An attitude of assumption is one of the most dangerous characteristics to have. Until you've actually accomplished something worthwhile for your organization, never assume you've arrived.

Man is the only creature whose head swells up when you pat him on the back.
—mc

Too much recognition can be as destructive as too much discipline.

If you feel everything is under control, you're not being objective enough.
—mc

Objectivity is the character of a leader that allows him or her to continually find that which needs improvement, correction, replacement, or promotion.

"Success is never final."
—Winston Churchill (1874–1965), English prime minister

There is never a time in today's economy where you can afford to feel like you're far enough ahead of the pack to relax your competitive edge.

72

"Teamwork is not always a good thing. A 'benevolent dictatorship' is sometimes necessary to break the lock on discussion and leadership. Decisions must be made."
　　—Robert A. Lutz, vice chairman, product development, General Motors

Some issues cannot be allowed to drag out forever. In today's economy, failure is occurring during the time it takes to make a decision.

"If we all did the things we were capable of, we would astound ourselves."
—Thomas Edison (1847–1931), inventor

It's an absolute truth that one never knows what he or she is capable of until the attempt has actually been made.

"You can't build a reputation on things you're going to do."
　　—Henry Ford (1863–1947), American auto manufacturer

You could spend a lifetime talking about all the things you're going to do before finally realizing that there's no time left to do any of it.

"Live your life so that your children can tell their children that you not only stood for something wonderful, you acted upon it."
—Dan Zadra, author, publisher

Acting on what you believe in and what you are really good at is part of a legacy that never dies in the minds of those who love and admire you.

There's nothing worse for your credibility than over-promising and then under-delivering.

　　　　　　　—mc

Be sure that when you tell someone you're going to do something, you're capable not only of doing it, but of exceeding their expectations.

You don't put growth in the bank. You put added dollars in the bank.

　　　　　　　—mc

Great numbers can disguise great problems. Be sure profit is profit.

"As you get older, don't slow down. Hurry up. There's less time left."
　　—Malcolm Forbes,
　　American publisher

Most individuals who lose their jobs after long, long years of service are not objective enough to realize that they had actually forfeited that position some time back by unconsciously starting to coast.

"Eighty percent of success is showing up."
　　—Woody Allen, author,
　　comedian, movie director

The least anyone can do is place themselves where opportunity can find them by just showing up for work.

Don't let your business take you where you have no business being.

　　　　　　　—mc

Monitor yourself, especially when there's no one else around. That's when you need self-discipline the most.

> *"Let's be out front, let's do it right, let's get it done now, and let's get on with it."*
> —Sam Walton (1918–1992), founder, Wal-Mart Stores

A sense of urgency is required if anyone is going to compete in today's economy and today's business environment. Change is occurring faster than at any time in our history, and you'll be held accountable by the speed of that change, whether you want to or not.

> *"If you're going to cry, do it with an agenda."*
> —Iyanla Vanzant, Christian author

Crying is often perceived by others to be a sign of weakness. In fact, it can mean joy, pain, frustration, sadness, or any one of many emotions. It can also be a sign of strength, when the one crying is simply taking a break to reload and prepare to start the battle all over again.

> *"You deal with people today who have plans about the plans they're planning on planning."*
> —Greg Ruka, Batman comic writer, author

Unless you have the element of planning in your strategic blueprint, your chances of getting outmaneuvered and just plain old "scooped" are 100 percent.

"Most bad decisions are made during good times."
—David Glass, chairman of the board, Wal-Mart Stores

The easiest thing to do when all is going well is to become complacent. It's during those good times when your focus should be the most intense, narrow, and disciplined.

"The more you sweat in peace, the less you bleed in war."
—Henry David Thoreau (1817–1862), author, poet

You must work harder to remain stable and successful when things are going well because that's when accountability will be at a premium.

An image is a shared vision, shared values, shared expectations, and shared purpose.
—unknown

There is no substitute for singing out of the same songbook when it comes to accomplishing common goals.

It's easier to make a good thing better than to make a bad thing good.
—mc

More money and productivity is spent redoing things than doing them right in the first place.

"In the game of life, even the fifty-yard-line seats don't interest me. I came to play."
—Dave Jackson, senior vice president, Wal-Mart Stores

The world is full of benchwarmers. There are never very many starters.

I think most anyone can face a crisis if there's no other alternative. It's the everyday stuff that most people struggle with.

—mc

There are so many choices available to people today, especially relative to ways of avoiding the simplest obligations, such as merely keeping an appointment. It may not be that important to you, but it may mean everything to the other person.

Do not confuse efforts with results. Sometimes doing your best is not good enough. You must do what's required.

—unknown

There are those who believe that putting forth your best effort is enough. In today's economy, there's no reward for being that naive.

"It's hard to imagine a more dangerous way of making decisions than by putting those decisions in the hands of people who pay no price for being wrong."
—Thomas Sowell, The Hoover Institution, Stanford University, Palo Alto, California

How we ever arrived at a place where we do not hold our government and corporate leaders, boards of directors, and financial managers accountable for the pillaging and plundering of our nation's people and its resources is beyond me.

CHAPTER EIGHT

Pride Goeth before the Fall

Pride is an excessive belief in one's own abilities to the degree that it interferes with their progress and the progress of those under their influence. It's also known as one of the "seven deadly sins," and the sin from which all other sins originate.

—Maxie Carpenter

William J. Clinton, forty-second
president of the United States

I've never positioned myself as either a Republican or a Democrat. If there is a classification into which one could place me politically, I guess it would be as an Independent. I've always voted for the person I felt was the best fit for the job based upon my instincts about the person and the country's health at that time. I voted for George H. W. Bush, Bill Clinton, and George W. Bush in each election accordingly, based upon that premise.

Many believe that a case can be made that the impeachment of Bill Clinton for personal malfeasance was pivotal in the evolution of the country's definition of leadership from one of inherent trust, integrity, and accountability to one of rationalization, tolerance, and apathy. I don't agree. I feel that our movement over time away from the basic, fundamental values upon which this country was founded and upon which the Constitution was created have been incremental and influenced by too much prosperity and a general attitude of personal entitlement rather than a striving for the common good.

When political individuals and parties are more interested in maintaining their positions of power than in the welfare of those they represent, as I believe is the case with far too many today, then the whole infrastructure suffers. In any institution, whether secular or religious, public or private, individual or family, one truth is absolute. Those who follow model the behavior of those who lead. The responsibility for a violation of trust and prideful behavior cannot be placed at the doorway of just one individual, one party, one nation, or one religion. We're all responsible.

Phrase

When common sense is at the mercy of pride, there is usually no contest.

—mc

Message

If more than twenty or so people tell you that you're dead, you might want to consider lying down.

Be humble. There isn't one single, new idea that isn't inspired by an old one.

—mc

In today's contemporary environment, there's a noticeable lack of respect for those who've come before to pave the way. It pains me to see that lack of respect not only overlooked, but in some organizations supported by leadership that is focused only on short-term gain.

People act like they're treated. How are you treating your people, and do you understand that people really do walk your talk?

—mc

Most leaders aren't conscious of the fact that they're being watched all the time. There is no break, no let-up, no lack of comparison, no time for complacency, and certainly no place to hide that cannot be found by people who really want to do what you're "modeling" them to do.

"The less justified a man is in claiming excellence for himself, the more ready he is to claim excellence for his nation, his religion, his race, or his cause."
—Eric Hoffer (1902–1983), American social philosopher

There is a time for focus on self, and that time is during the search of how best to equip one's self to serve others.

Mutiny usually occurs be-low the deck.

—mc

If you're so proud that you want to spend all your time on the top, then you shouldn't be so surprised by what's going on at the bottom.

"It's what we learn after we know it all that counts."
—Mrs. A. C. Carlson, Minnesota delegate to the Republican National Convention (1932)

The minute you stop the process of educating your-self, you begin the process of becoming dispensable.

A great character element to have is the patience to be rewarded.

—mc

Pride encourages a sense of urgency that requires imme-diate gratification, and yet history has proven that any-thing of value only becomes more so with maturity.

Inverted leadership means that you have to have served first before you can lead.

—mc

Pride can encourage one to want more than one is ca-pable of handling. There is tremendous value in taking all the steps required in the process, because any activity that adds more knowledge to your personal library en-sures longevity.

The second you start feeling proud of yourself, someone will surely pass you by.
　　　　　　　—unknown

There are many self-fulfilling behaviors one can model that will define their future very accurately. One of those is pride.

"Everyone is a genius at least once a year. The real geniuses simply try to have their bright ideas closer together."
　—George Lichtenberg (1742–1799), German Christian author

A sense of humility is the greatest asset you can use as leverage against the presence of too much pride.

"No one can make you feel inferior without your consent."
　—Eleanor Roosevelt (1884–1962), First Lady of the United States

Pride is fueled only by a lack of resistance.

"Love your enemies. It makes them so damn mad."
　—Mark Twain (1835–1910), humorist and author

Another great asset to use as leverage against too much pride is a continual display of sincerity regardless of the circumstances. A prideful person can hold out only so long against a very sincere and moral person.

"If you've never skinned your knees, you may not have learned enough."
—Tom Coughlin, executive vice chairman, board of directors, Wal-Mart Stores

Failure is the great educator. Advancing through life without too many consequences can have disastrous results at a time when you need them the very least.

Never have so much pride that you are unwilling to consider changing a decision, especially when everyone around you is telling you it was a bad decision.

—mc

Pride is the greatest of all sins because it is the father and mother of all sin.

You only get one chance at a first impression.

—unknown

Studies have shown that the first impression one receives of another is the impression that remains prevalent from the beginning of the relationship until its conclusion.

You never lose. You just run out of time.

—mc

The pride someone takes in never having failed in a major objective pales in comparison to the pride another takes in knowing that winning is actually the continual pursuit of an objective.

84

Learning the hard way is not a bad thing.

—mc

There is a lot to be said for experiencing some difficulty, some obstacle, some disappointment, or even some failure on occasion. It's the essence of finally experiencing success and prevents pride from dominating the process.

Don't take yourself so seriously. There were others here before you, and there will surely be others here after you.

—mc

It's healthy to have respect for those who made your way easier to navigate, and it's healthy to understand that you have a legacy to leave for those coming behind you.

"It's a fine thing to rise above pride, and you must have pride to do so."
—George Bernanos (1888–1948), French novelist and political writer

Pride is not an unhealthy trait to have if it prevents you from submitting to the willful pride of those who do not have your best interests at heart.

"Generosity is giving more than you can, and pride is taking less than you need."
—Kahlil Gibran (1883–1931), Lebanese-born American author and poet

This is as short, simple, and accurate as it gets. If we really thought of how we managed others in relation to this definition, I wonder how much more consistent we would be.

CHAPTER NINE

Attitude vs. Mindset

Be sure you know what an attitude is before you accuse another of having one. Very often, the problem we accuse someone of having is the one we refuse to own.

—Maxie Carpenter

The author and his faithful red wagon

You would not believe what this wagon was capable of. I could haul a couple of my sisters down the road at the speed of sound, or at least until one of them fell out anyway. There was no list of groceries that Mom could give me that I couldn't get in that wagon. It seemed as if I could haul a cord of firewood in one trip. There wasn't a hill steep enough, a ditch wide enough, or a creek too deep that I couldn't navigate with that wagon. It never broke down, never failed to go the distance, and because it had those hard polyurethane tires, never had a flat. I took that thing with me everywhere I went. It wasn't a coincidence that I felt pretty much like I could handle anything as long as I had that wagon with me. I couldn't tell you what eventually happened to that wagon, but I'm certain it had a lot to do with shaping the mindset and the attitude of a very young boy.

Phrase

One should take a child's philosophy to heart. They never despise a bubble when it bursts. They immediately set to work to blow another one.
—unknown

"If you occasionally fall, and we all do, just be sure to fall forward."
—Dan Zadra, author, publisher, consultant

Message

It's much easier to have an attitude of defeat than it is to be eternally optimistic. However, the latter is much healthier and more rewarding in the long run.

If you actually try this physically, it's much easier to get up from a position of having fallen forward than it is from a position of having fallen backward. It's a philosophical mindset as well.

"It's only possible to live happily ever after on a day-to-day basis."
　—Margaret Bonano, author

There is no guarantee of tomorrow for any of us. As far as we know, our lives could be dramatically altered in the course of a very few seconds. It happens to someone every second of every minute of every hour of every day.

"Always bear in mind that your own resolution to succeed is more important than any other one thing."
　—Abraham Lincoln, sixteenth president of the United States

I've always wondered how it was that once I finally resolved to do something, it seemed as if events started conspiring to reward my resolve.

Plan ahead. It wasn't raining when Noah built the ark.
　　　　　—unknown

I'm amazed at the fact that 75 percent of new businesses fail in the first year because the desire to get up and running took priority over the process of planning ahead for success.

"There are no hard and fast rules around here. We're trying to accomplish something."
　　　—Thomas Edison
　　(1847–1931), inventor

The mindset that values innovation, creativeness, and imagination should always entertain the idea of stretching existing parameters, guidelines, and assumptions.

"Hats off to the past, coats off to the future."
—Baron Rothschild
(1845–1934), banker

The contributions of those who've come before us are to be considered, honored, and respected. They're not boundaries beyond which those coming after are not to go.

You're the product of what's happening to you, and at the end of the day that's what you have.
—mc

It's foolish to rationalize about what causes your life to be influenced in a manner other than what you desire. Be realistic enough to understand that it's a product of the choices you make.

A person usually runs out of "want to" before their customer runs out of "need."
—unknown

Never underestimate the hunger and curiosity of the American consumer.

"I could not sleep when I got on the hunt for a new idea, until I had caught it. This was a kind of passion with me, and it has stuck with me since."
—Abraham Lincoln, sixteenth president of the United States

A prominent characteristic of anyone who accomplished anything defined as great by existing parameters is perseverance. Lincoln had it in spades.

"You're successful the moment you start moving towards a worthwhile goal."
—Charles B. Carlson, author, investor

Being idle, standing in place, or being defensive rather than offensive seldom accomplishes one's goals or aspirations.

"In communities where men build ships for their own sons to fish or fight from, quality is never a problem."
—J. William Deville, author

Any product perceived by the consumer as one of consistent, dependable quality that exceeds expectation time and time again will find a supplier with this mindset applied to every product each and every time.

"Mental toughness means knowing that the decisions you make sometimes hurt those closest to you. It's also the ability to know that you're human and that you will make mistakes."
—Tom Laughlin, former Green Beret, U.S. Army

The most difficult thing for any great leader to do is maintain objectivity with those closest to them. After that, the most difficult thing to do is to forgive oneself.

Attitude is entering the Indianapolis 500 with a Volkswagen and expecting to win.
—mc

Knowing the odds is half the battle, but allowing those odds to defeat the purpose of your mission is unacceptable.

"Anyone with a new idea is a crank, until the idea succeeds."
—Mark Twain (1835–1910), author

It's amazing how behaviors and attitudes change towards someone when an idea that seems absolutely ludicrous is given the chance to work.

"I'm a great believer in luck, and I find the harder I work, the more I have of it."
—Thomas Jefferson, third president of the United States

This is a fact that has forever been and will forever be. Try it and you'll be amazed at what happens.

Forget your failures only long enough to be successful again.
—mc

Success is inversely proportionate to the amount of time spent dwelling upon failure and is directly proportionate to the amount of time spent dwelling upon trying again.

The ability to be taught has nothing to do with age and everything to do with attitude.
—mc

I've known some of the most talented people in the world who were not as successful as they should have been simply because they refused to be taught.

The workplace is not the best place to have too much of an attitude of "volunteerism."

—mc

If you volunteer yourself for projects that you're not accountable for to the degree that the ones you are accountable for suffer, then you can volunteer yourself right out of a job.

"If your failure rate is one in a million, what do you tell that one customer?"

—IBM slogan

Everyone counts. No amount of success, wealth, or recognition should breed complacency to the degree that even one single customer or employee doesn't count.

"Anything I've ever done that ultimately was worthwhile initially scared me to death."

—Betty Bender, author, organizational consultant

If you never make the attempt, you'll never know how great you could have become. To me, it's the ultimate tragedy.

"The significant problems we face cannot be solved at the same level of thinking we were at when we created them."

—Albert Einstein (1879–1955), German mathematician

I think we've all heard it said before that the definition of insanity is doing the same things and expecting different results.

"Things may come to those who wait, but only the things left by those who hustle."
　　—Abraham Lincoln, sixteenth
　　president of the United States

If you don't want it bad enough, someone else always will. More importantly, they'll want it first.

"Too much quality can ruin you. When was the last time you chose a place to eat based on a bad experience you had rather than what's perceived to be positive?"
　　—Robert Lutz, vice chairman,
　　　　product development,
　　　　　General Motors

You only remember the negative effects of a bad experience, not the positive. Unfortunately, it's the essence of human nature.

"How could anything be more fun than loving what you do and feeling that it matters?"
　　　　—Katharine Graham
　　　　(1917–2001), CEO,
The Washington Post Company

If you don't, you need to rethink your future right now.

"Money never starts the idea; it's the idea that starts the money."
　　—W. J. Cameron, vice president, Ford Motor Company

Do you really have the end in sight, or are you just spinning your wheels?

We're all born common; no one has to stay that way.
—unknown

I truly believe that you can become whatever you want to. It's simply a matter of resolve and effort.

"Creativity has nothing to do with 'casual day.' There is value in dressing for the task. There must be discipline which builds cohesion."
—Robert Lutz, vice chairman, product development, General Motors

Your attitude towards a chosen goal can either be lax or disciplined. I also believe that the way you dress is as important to shaping your mindset as it is to influencing how others perceive you.

There is always a gap between what you desire and what you can accomplish.
—mc

Be smart enough to recognize the gap and aggressive enough to find out how to bridge it.

"The goal of business is not only to make money. Why subordinate everything to the purpose of making money?"
—Robert Lutz, vice chairman, product development, General Motors

Unless you really have a passion for what you're doing to make money, prepare to limit your expectations.

"There is more to life than simply increasing its speed."
—Mahatma Gandhi (1869–1948), Indian philosopher, religious leader

With the speed of change in today's corporate environment, understanding this principle would really simplify a lot of complex issues.

"People don't give a hoot about who made the original 'whatzit.' They only want to know who makes the best one."
—Howard W. Newton, author

Always be aware of where your focus should be; keep it simple and relevant.

CHAPTER 10

Relationships

Relationships are the foundation of any accomplishment, whether it's considered small or large in significance, or whether it's personal or public in nature.

—Maxie Carpenter

Johnny Mack and Jackie

In today's society, it's not difficult at all for relationships of any kind to be broken at any time for any reason, with little thought given to the long-term effects upon those who depend upon those relationships for support and development. We see it happen with increasing frequency in both the public sector—with governmental trust and educational provision—to the private sector, with corporate and professional commitments, religious authority, and marriages. All too often, the desire for personal satisfaction overrides concern for the common good, and accountability is ransomed for rationalization. Over the course of my parents' lives together, there were many reasons for which they could have decided to break the relationship and go their separate ways. Those reasons are not any more unique or different than the reasons for which marriages are broken today, believe me. Mercy, having six children was enough of a reason by itself, some would say. The key message here is that they chose not to do so. They placed unconditional love for those who depended upon them for support and development ahead of their own personal desires and self-interest. In the last year of Dad's life, he said that the accomplishment he was proudest of was that he raised a good family and that he didn't leave any debts behind for my mother. I can only aspire to be that fortunate.

Phrase	Message
"Trust each other again and again, and when the trust level gets high enough, people transcend apparent limits and discover new abilities of which they were previously unaware." —David Armistead, founder and president, Nova Communication	When trust is absent, communication is impossible. Without trust, there can be no great commissions, great deeds, great breakthroughs, or great accomplishments.
Offer someone a piece of gum and they'll move in tomorrow. —mc	You'd be amazed at the great events and relationships this simple little gesture inspires.

Building a relationship is comparable to managing a checking account. If your deposits are always greater than your withdrawals, you never have to worry about the balance. Conversely, if withdrawals exceed deposits, you're bankrupt.

—mc

How relationships are managed and invested in determines their profitability.

"The ultimate test of a relationship is to disagree but to hold hands."
—Alexander Penney, author

Depending on the severity of the disagreement, this can be absolutely the hardest thing to do. Trust me, I've tried it. It challenges the sincerity with which you forgive.

We're not leaving here until there's a lot of blood or a lot of love.

—mc

There are times when an issue has got to be melted down one way or another, especially if it's critical to your survival.

It never improves a relationship to keep score or to take such delight in being right that you forget how it feels to be wrong.

—mc

After winning an argument, the best thing you can do is apologize.

Relationships are not for those short on commitment or long on material rewards.

—mc

When a relationship becomes valued more for what it can provide in the way of advantage, position, financial resource, or other personal gain, then it can no longer be defined as a relationship. It's either a political alliance or a foolish misplacement of trust.

When trust is shot, communication is impossible.

—mc

Trust is the most empowering emotion in our known universe. Complete trust inspires complete communication that lifts everyone in the relationship to complete success.

"A relationship is the state of being connected or interrelated; the relation connecting or binding participants in a relationship; a state of affairs existing between those having relations or dealings."
—Merriam-Webster's Online

Once you understand the true meaning or definition of anything, it can influence your outcome in a more positive way. The same holds true for relationships.

It's not a relationship if you're always wondering what the other person's motives are. It's a crapshoot.

—mc

If you're simply gambling that "this one will be the right one," then, just as in gambling, prepare to remain in anticipation for the duration of the relationship, wondering if you're ever going to win or not.

"By people we are broken, and by people we are put together again."

—John Drakeford, author

Most relationships suffer from the practice of avoidance. If we continue to hide relative to negative influences or issues, then the chances of survival are very limited. The other person is your best resource for a resolution.

"Often the difference between a successful marriage and a mediocre one consists of leaving about three or four things a day unsaid."

—Harlan Miller, author

Enough said.

When you graduate, it doesn't mean that the homework stops. It just means that the environment changed from school to real life.

—mc

This is more so in relationships than anywhere else. When you stop studying in an effort to improve yourself at work and at home, then your chances of failing at both are substantially enhanced.

"Goals bring harmony to your life."
—Dr. Paul Faulkner, director, Marriage and Family Institute, Austin, Texas

When there are common beliefs, common values, and common goals, relationships flourish. Even one potential opportunity for either party to be going in a different direction should not be overlooked.

"Too often, a sense of loyalty depends on admiration, and if we can't admire it's difficult to be loyal."
—Aimee Buchanan, artist, author, worship leader

Think about how this relates to someone you happen to be working for right now. If you think about it, it makes all the sense in the world.

"The most important single ingredient in success is to know how to get along with people."
—Theodore Roosevelt, twenty-sixth president of the United States

Did you know that getting along with people is an art form that can be studied? If you understand the four existing personality types and how to categorize people accordingly, your chances for succeeding are very much enhanced.

CHAPTER 11

"Johnny Mack"

Son, I want you to make sure that no one in the family fights over anything after I'm gone. I know there's not a hell of a lot left, but at least all the bills are paid and your mother won't have any financial stuff to worry over.

—John Mack Carpenter

The statement above was typical of my dad. He always had a somewhat jaded sense of humor that I think may have been typical for that generation. At times, I'm aware of reflecting that same perspective myself. I think it comes from the difficulty of adjusting to a societal norm that has evolved over time from one where everyone worked towards the good of the whole to one where most work towards the good of the individual. In other words, it's an environment that's moved from a mindset of good intentions to one of entitlements. But as an eternal optimist, I believe that everything comes around in time based upon human behavior. As an eternal

Christian, I believe there is a greater reward that ultimately comes as well, based upon the same premise.

I know that the behaviors of most people have a certain significance of some kind. Yet, I'm not sure why I began collecting this assortment of observations. I'm not even certain when I started. In the beginning, if you were to have asked me if I had the intent at some point in time of writing this kind of publication, I would have been surprised at the suggestion of such an idea. I'd never considered myself a person of literature to the point of being able to produce anything that would be comparable to the many quality publications I've read over the course of my life.

So, when did the idea for this book occur to me? As I look back over the last few years since my father passed, I've been able to understand that his death influenced me in a way that I was unable to comprehend at the time. I was actually at a crossroads in my own life and didn't realize it. Even if I had, I don't think I would have taken the time to deal with it, had it not been for my father. He was given about one year to live from the time he was diagnosed with lung cancer in December 1995. At the beginning of that year, I was preparing to transition from a corporate human resources position to a corporate operations position. That meant I would be traveling extensively again, which I'd done for twenty years before accepting a move to corporate in the first place. In other words, I was continuing the process of climbing the corporate ladder because that's what was expected of me, and I'd always done what was expected of me. At that time, it was necessary to tell the company that I couldn't make that transition because of Dad's diagnosis. I wanted to spend his last year being available for him and my mother in whatever way was necessary. Although that was foremost in my mind, it was also true that I was not looking forward to traveling again. My kids were, in my opinion, at an age when I felt that my influence in their lives was going to be the most critical. My wife felt that I'd been unhappy for some time. She was seeing that unhappiness reflected in my behavior at home, to which I was oblivious because of what had always been a single-minded focus on doing the very best job I could at doing what was expected of me. Additionally, watching my father suffer with so much pain in that last year, watching my mother struggle to maintain some sense of normalcy on a daily basis, and watching how each of my five sisters struggled with Dad's illness in their own way were revelations for me.

From the time I'd left high school, I'd always been basically removed to a degree from the rest of the family. I'd been going to school and then working, always working. I'd also grown spiritually distant in my relationship with God. This had been a priority for most of my life, more so when my children were born, and increasingly of critical concern as I accelerated my career.

Additionally, without realizing it, seeing Dad almost daily during his last year allowed me to grow in more ways as a man than I could ever have imagined. Watching him face the end of his life with the full knowledge of approximately when it was going to end was an example of courage I'll likely never see again, and I was profoundly changed because of it. Can you imagine being able to say you learned more about being a man at middle age than you'd ever learned previously in your life?

I made the decision literally in the space of one hour to conclude a twenty-seven-year career. I realized that I was no longer considered the asset I'd been in the past. I was not effective for my wife, I was not effective for my children, I was not effective for my extended family, I was not effective for myself, and I certainly wasn't effective for God.

I want to be clear here that this is not a cleansing of the soul, a purging of the demons, an admission of guilt, a declaration of independence, a cry of freedom, or any one of a number of vehicles that many use to make a life statement. If it's perceived that way, that certainly isn't my intent.

Maybe I'm just catching up to saying all the things I've felt for some time and wouldn't because it was more important to do what I thought was expected of me than to simply be myself. Maybe I'm trying to prove that not having a college degree doesn't mean I'm not capable of doing great things. Maybe I'm trying to show my family and others how much my father really meant to me. Maybe I'm trying to show others that there really is a true, decent, simple, caring, effective way to communicate with people that has more to its mission than succeeding at someone else's expense. Maybe I'm trying to do all of the above. For whatever reason, I'm a better person for having done so.

Tribute

I WISH YOU COULD HAVE KNOWN MY DAD

I really wish you could have known my dad;
    his life was a work of art.
He always seemed to know just when and how to play his part.
He'd give a subtle look, or a simple "hey," or a sigh of
    resignation.
Maybe a wink, maybe a smile, you never needed an explanation.

My dad had his vices, as most of us knew;
Not too many really, just a very few.
He smoked to excess, and he loved a game of gin.
As some of us know, he took a drink now and then.

Dad loved to tell stories of his life with his friends.
He never treated anyone as a means to an end.
He always gave more than he ever received.
He always shot straight and he never deceived.

Dad worked all his life, he'd be proud to tell you.
There wasn't a task that he said "I just won't do."
He always worked hard, stayed long, and was strong.
Dad knew that not doing so was too often wrong.

My mom provided support and endless perseverance,
She and Dad raised a family of amazing endurance.
Five girls and a boy, and we've all grown up strong.
We've thrived in the shadow of my dad's empowering song.

He praised, he encouraged, he scolded, and he pushed us.
Even to the time that he returned to the dust.
Time has always proved it again and again.
There was no substitute for the wisdom he gave.

His memory will live on through the years as we strive.
We'll set the example for our kids in their lives.
I'm not one to boast or necessarily brag.
But I really wish you could have known my dad.

This tribute was written by Maxie Van Carpenter, son of John Mack Carpenter, and read to those in attendance at the celebration of his life on December 12, 1996.

Bibliography

Allison, Mary Ann. 1986. *Managing Up and Down*. Simon & Schuster.

Bach, Richard. 1989. *A Gift of Wings*. Dell Books.

Barton, Bruce. 1924. *The Man Nobody Knows*. The Bobbs-Merrill Company.

Boyd, Thomas A. 2002. *Charles F. Kettering: A Biography*. Beard Group.

Carlson, Charles B. 2000. *The Smart Investor's Survival Guide: The Nine Laws of Successful Investing in a Volatile Market*. Doubleday.

Davis, Joann. 2003. *The Best Things in Life Aren't Things: Celebrating What Matters Most*. Beacon Press.

De Pree, Max. 1993. *Leadership Jazz*. Doubleday.

Diehl, William E. 1991. *The Monday Connection: A Spirituality of Competence, Affirmation, and Support in the Workplace*. Harper Collins.

Emerson, Ralph Waldo. 2003. *The Spiritual Emerson: Essential Writings by Ralph Waldo Emerson*. Beacon Press.

Faulkner, Paul. 1986. *Making Things Right When Things Go Wrong*. Sweet Publishing.

Feather, William. 1949. *The Business of Life: American Biography Series*. Reprint Services Corporation.

Francis of Sales. 1998. *Finding God's Will for You*. Sophia Institute of Printing.

Gibran, Kahlil. 1995. *The Treasured Writings of Kahlil Gibran*. Book Sales, Reprint Edition.

Graves, Stephen R., and Thomas G. Addington. 2002. *Behind the Bottom Line*. Jossey Bass.

Herman, Roger, and The Herman Group. 1999. *Keeping Good People*. Oakhill Press.

Hill, Napoleon. 1937. *Think and Grow Rich*. Fawcett Books.

Holmes, John H. 1932. *A Sensible Man's View of Religion*. Columbia University Press.

Hubbard, Elbert. 1999. *Elbert Hubbard's Scrapbook: Containing the Inspired and Inspiring Selections Gathered during a Lifetime of Discriminating Reading for His Own Use*. Firebird Press.

Humes, James C. 1982. *The Wit & Wisdom of Abraham Lincoln*. Random House Value Publishing, Inc.

Lao-tzu. 1986. *Tao of Leadership: Lao-tzu's Tao Te Ching Adapted for a New Age*. Humanics Publishing Group.

Magee, Bryan. 1997. *The Philosophy of Schopenhauer*. Oxford University Press.

Moawad, Bob. 1991. *Whatever It Takes: A Journey into the Heart of Human Achievement*. Gift Edition. Compendium, Inc.

Peters, Tom. 1988. *In Search of Excellence: Lessons from America's Best-Run Companies*. Warner Books.

Peterson, Wilfred A. 1991. *The Art of Creative Thinking*. Hay House.

Phillips, Donald T. 1993. *Lincoln on Leadership: Executive Strategies for Tough Times*. Warner Books.

Schopenhauer, Arthur. 1818. *The World as Will and Representation*. Abridged Edition. Everyman's Library.

Shackleton, Earnest H. 1999. *South: The Endurance Expedition*. Signet.

Tice, Lou. 1997. *Personal Coaching for Results: How to Mentor and Inspire Others to Amazing Growth*. Thomas Nelson.

Trimble, Vance H. 1990. *Sam Walton: The Inside Story of America's Richest Man*. The Penguin Group.

Twain, Mark, Howard G. Baetzhold, and Joseph G. McCullough. 1996. *The Bible According to Mark Twain: Irreverent Writings on Eden, Heaven, and the Flood by America's Master Satirist*. Touchstone Books.

Vanzant, Iyanla. 2000. *Yesterday I Cried: Celebrating the Lessons of Living and Loving*. Fireside.

Walton, Sam M., and John Huey. 1992. *Sam Walton: Made in America, My Story*. Doubleday.

Wheatley, Margaret, and Myron Kellner-Rogers. 1999. *A Simpler Way*. Barrett-Koehler Publishing.

Zadra, Dan. 2001. *Together We Can: Celebrating the Power of a Team and a Dream*. Compendium, Inc.

About the Author

Maxie Carpenter is recognized for his expertise in the areas of human resources, training and communications, and store operations. During his twenty-seven-year career with Wal-Mart Stores Inc., he pioneered programs specific to creating simple and relevant operational processes, and assisted in the creation and implementation of mentoring, succession planning, and people measurement processes that helped identify Wal-Mart as world-class relevant to the depth and quality of its management pool and the retention of its workforce. Mr. Carpenter is also recognized as an accomplished public speaker and an authority on the subject of corporate culture.

As a member of Wal-Mart's corporate Benefits Development Committee, he was instrumental in the creation, development, and implementation of health care benefits for Wal-Mart's domestic workforce, which numbered approximately 1 million associates. He also lobbied in Washington, representing the interests of company associates relevant to health care legislation.

As a member of Wal-Mart's corporate Profit Sharing Committee, he was instrumental in making decisions relevant to leveraging approximately $429 million in contributions to the company profit sharing and 401(k) plans for maximum return on investment.

As a member of Wal-Mart's Governmental Affairs Committee, he was responsible for working with the Public Affairs Division in representing the interests of the domestic operating division relevant to federal influence and compliance.

As a member of Wal-Mart's Diversity Action Committee, he was instrumental in creating, developing, and implementing diversity initiatives with the goal of advancing the interests of minorities and women, combined with educating the overall corporate population to the advantages associated with supporting diversity.

As a member of Wal-Mart's corporate Strategic Planning Committee, he participated in the company's first (and ensuing) comprehensive, five-year strategic planning session that included representatives from every operating division. This plan became the cornerstone of a process that helped the company's leadership understand the correlation over time of long-range planning to results, especially in the areas of asset management, retention of people, and the setting of realistic, attainable goals.

As a member of Wal-Mart's corporate Policy & Procedure Committee, he was instrumental for reviewing, modifying, creating, and implementing company policy for the entire domestic operating division, which required a comprehensive understanding of the broad range of all legal implications involved. He was recognized by the company as an expert resource to the legal community in matters relating to policy and procedure.

As a member of the Food Advisory Board of Western Michigan University in Kalamazoo, Michigan, which specialized in the education of food management and supervision, he acted as liaison, faculty advisor, and conference and classroom speaker to the academic community, representing the interests of the company relevant to curriculum, recruitment, and life enrichment for students.

As a member of the Board of Trustees for The University of Texas–Pan American in Edinburg, Texas, he was instrumental in the evolution of the company's relationship with constituents of the Rio Grande Valley, resulting in improved recruitment and retention of Hispanic students from a success rate of less than 10 percent to over

85 percent. The university enjoys the distinction of having one of the largest enrollments of Hispanic students in the United States.

Currently Mr. Carpenter serves in the following capacities:

• Member, the Board of Advisors for the Herman Group of Greensboro, North Carolina, an established consulting and public speaking firm specializing in workforce issues, future trends forecasting, and employee retention.

• Member, the Board of Advisors for the International Assembly for Collegiate Business Education, a specialized accrediting body for business degree programs in higher education.

• Founding member and vice president emeritus of the Benton County Charter School Organization, Inc. (which created one of the first charter schools in the state of Arkansas).

Areas of Expertise
Human resources
Store operations
Training and communications

Education
Harding College, Searcy, Arkansas
University of Arkansas, Fayetteville, Arkansas
Kennedy-Western University, Thousand Oaks, California

Background Summary
2003–Present
Senior Partner, Diversified Retail Solutions, LLC
2000–2003
MVC Advisory Resource, Inc., founder and president
1996–2000
Wal-Mart Stores, Inc., Supercenter Division, vice president of people (HR), training and communications
1993–1996
Wal-Mart Stores, Inc., Domestic Division, vice president of people (HR), training and communications

1992–1993
Wal-Mart Stores, Inc., operations coordinator, Western United States
1973–1992
Wal-Mart Stores, Inc., Store Field Operations

Current Interests
Chairman, Corporate Committee, Circle of Life Hospice & Palliative Care, Inc., Springdale, Arkansas
Community group shepherd, Fellowship Bible Church of Northwest AR, Lowell, Arkansas
Volunteer counselor, Small Business Association of Counselors (SCORE), U.S. Small Business Administration, Rogers, Arkansas Chapter
Vice president emeritus, Benton County Charter School Organiza tion, Inc., Rogers, Arkansas

Anyone's Five-Chapter Autobiography in One Page

Chapter 1
I walk down the street.
There's a deep hole in the sidewalk.
I fall in.
I'm lost. I'm hopeless.
It isn't my fault.
It takes forever to find a way out.

Chapter 2
I walk down the same street.
There's a deep hole in the sidewalk.
I pretend I don't see it.
I fall in again.
I can't believe I'm in the same place.
But, it isn't my fault.

Chapter 3
I walk down the same street.
There's a deep hole in the sidewalk.
I see it there.
I still fall in. It's a habit.
My eyes are open.
I know where I am.
It's my fault.
I get out immediately.

Chapter 4
I walk down the same street.
There's a deep hole in the sidewalk.
I walk around it.

Chapter 5
I walk down another street.

Source:
 Portia Nelson, "Autobiography in Five
 Short Chapters,"
 New Man, March 2002.
 Reprinted with persmission.

Acknowledgments

There are so many people that come and go in our lives on a daily basis that it would be impossible to name them all. In fact, there are some whose names may never be known. Maybe their contribution seemed of such an insignificant nature that the names weren't necessary; someone sitting next to you on a plane, who offered you a piece of gum; a cab driver, who didn't charge you for giving him the wrong address; a hotel consigliore, who didn't accept a tip because you didn't have change for a twenty; a hospital nurse, who brought you a sedative at 3:00 a.m. because you were in so much pain you couldn't sleep, and made sure you weren't charged for it; a counselor, who listened to you for an extra hour and didn't charge you because your insurance wouldn't have covered it; a mechanic, who repaired a problem you didn't know you had and didn't ask to be paid; and I could go on and on.

Then there are those, who, in the course of their lives, may or may never get any significant recognition, but who made such significant contributions to my life that their importance cannot be ignored and I will never forget their names. There are some that I've lost contact with and have no idea what's become of them, and then there are others, who are still contributing to my life today. Since I consider this book to be somewhat unique in content and format, then allow me to be also somewhat unique in this acknowledgement by recognizing those people.

Ed Robertson, Wal-Mart District Manager, Tulsa, Oklahoma: he actually listened when I said I had something more to offer and helped me have the opportunity to do so.

Walter Buchanan, Church of Christ Minister, Waxahatchie, Texas: a true disciple of Christ, who persevered through more diversity than most I've known and never wavered from his trust in God.

Al Wisenfels, Wal-Mart District Manager Retired, Lufkin, Texas: the cornerstone of his management style was a wonderful sense of humor that influenced me tremendously.

Mickey Robinson, Wal-Mart District Manager Deceased, Tulsa, Oklahoma: he gave me some "tough love" by telling me not to ever call him again if all I was going to do was complain. It was a lesson I never forgot.

Arlen Brown, Store Manager, Greenville, Mississippi: he taught me the value of being able to make the hard call and being willing and able to stand for the criticism of doing so.

Ophelia "Tilly" Stark, Store Keeper, Hardy, Arkansas: the first woman, aside from my mother and my grandmother, who loved me as one of her own and influenced me with her discipline and perseverance.

Maud White, 5th Grade Teacher, Hardy, Arkansas: she "dressed to the nines" every day and influenced me with how you present and articulate yourself as professionally as possible.

Lynn Garner, Junior High Basketball Coach, Hardy, Arkansas: he taught me the value of effort by telling me that it didn't matter if you were playing your grandmother, you played as hard as you could.

Coach Robert Lewis, High School Basketball Coach, Bentonville, Arkansas: he sat down beside me, put his arm around my shoulder, and told me he was proud of me right after we'd lost by two points to Subiaco Academy in the Benton County Championship Tournament. I'll never forget that.

Suzanne Alford, Executive Vice President, HEB Stores, San Antonio, Texas: the first human resource professional I ever worked with, who influenced me to focus on working through people as a profession rather than as a means to an end.

Oradell White, former member, Church of Christ, Bentonville, Arkansas: my mother's best friend when I was eighteen (18), who, with the greatest act of courage I've ever personally witnessed, influenced me to stand for what you believe in no matter what.

Marie Soileau, housewife and friend, Washington, Louisiana: she taught me the meaning of hospitality by opening her home to me and my wife at a time when it became a place of comfort and refuge. She made the best "shrimp etoufe" I've ever eaten.

Sandra Castille, Wal-Mart office associate and friend, Opelousas, Louisiana: she was always there with a smile on her face, a cheerful "Hello, Mr. C.", and amazing loyalty and support.

Ramona Dugas, Wal-Mart office associate and friend, Opelousas, Louisiana: she was a confidante I could always go to and ask "What do you think?" Her wisdom never failed to influence me.

Jerome Schieder, Wal-Mart District Manager Retired, Jefferson City, Missouri: the best man at my wedding and a friend at a time when we were the only two friends each other had.

William "Mac" McMorris, Wal-Mart Regional Personnel Manager, Bentonville, Arkansas: a groomsman in my wedding and a friend at a time and place where our relationship was invaluable for both of us, both personally and professionally.

William Babb & Jeff Spencer, college teammates and friends, Harding College, Searcy, Arkansas: Bill was from Dallas, Texas, and Jeff was from Pocahontas, Arkansas, and we were the shortest guys on the basketball team. We went everywhere and did everything together and they were a part of two of the best years of my life.

Gary Wendike, high school friend, Bentonville, Arkansas: we were two guys immersed in a spiritual upbringing that influenced us towards a common characteristic; having reputations as always staying on the straight and narrow no matter what, which left us in the minority most of the time when it came to the rest of our school friends. That, and our common interest in music, forged a friendship that was invaluable.

Kendall Schwindt, Wal-Mart Senior Vice President Retired, Rogers, Arkansas: he was tougher than a boot nail and more intense and focused than just about anyone I've ever worked with. But he was always willing to stand in the gap if he believed in you and he was always willing to be challenged, something most leaders just don't get.

Bonnie Wolf, consultant, Atlanta, Georgia: she influenced me with an amazing faith and endurance after the loss of a son that would have paralyzed most people I know.

Terry Thurman, retired military and friend, Rogers, Arkansas: he influenced me with such a display of character and fortitude in the face of unbelievable and undeserved criticism that I will always marvel at how he managed it.

Ruth Ann Fields, Tulsa, Oklahoma; Annette LaLonde, Modesto, California; Wendy Turner, Colorado Springs, Colorado; Pam Shook, Cave Springs, Arkansas; Stephanie Garrard, Las Vegas, Nevada, Kris Weakley, Bentonville, Arkansas: these individuals were my administrative assistants at various times over the course of my entire career and each of their contributions was unique to the degree that I couldn't have succeeded without any of them. Though they probably didn't know it, I learned more from each of them than they ever learned from me.

Oddie Straight, small business owner and operator, Springdale, Arkansas: this man and his wife never miss a day of work that I'm aware of and they are elite business people in that truly understand the value of a customer. They understand that treating customers in terms of a relationship influences your profitability and survival more than anything else.

Doug Parker, Senior Vice President, Commercial and Private Banking Group Manager, Regions Bank, Rogers, Arkansas: this gentleman recognized a vision and took a risk, especially when more visible financial players wouldn't give that idea the time of day because it was too politically sensitive. Today a vision that is influencing an entire state's educational perspective is flourishing in large part because of him.

Chuck Reeves, Sr., friend and neighbor, Rogers, Arkansas: this gentleman goes down in my record book as one of the most genuine, friendly, and caring individuals I've ever been honored to know. His wife, his son, and his son's family are absolutely cut from the same cloth and they all bless my life on a regular basis.

Mickey Rapier, Worship Leader, Fellowship Bible Church, Lowell, Arkansas: this man walks with God in way that can only be described as incomparable. It's a walk that is modeled every second of every minute of every hour of every day of his life. It's a philosophy of life that constantly amazes me and causes me to aspire to that standard.

Matt Loveless, Wal-Mart Store Manager and friend, Rogers, Arkansas: this young man considers me his mentor, yet what I've learned from him could produce another book about friendship, humility, enthusiasm, perseverance, thankfulness, and leadership.

Kathy Johnson, housewife and friend, Tulsa, Oklahoma: this lady and her entire family (Pam, Debbie, Marsha, the brothers, their Mother, their Father now deceased) have been such a tremendous influence over the course of my life because of their loyalty to family, their loyalty to friends, and most importantly, the joy and laughter they always shared as a family with those who happened to cross their paths.

Cindy Acree, small business owner and friend, Aurora, Colorado: the only living survivor of epilepsy surgery in the United States, who has inspired and amazed me with a pursuit of life after near death that has produced a wonderful family, a thriving business, and a continual desire to help others.

Rhonda Carpenter, sister, Bentonville, Arkansas: I can think of few people who've experienced more bad breaks in their life, yet she continues to forge ahead, persevere, and maintain a sense of humor and faith that's amazing in it's honesty. She's inspired me without ever knowing it.

Melania Ross, sister, Tulsa, Oklahoma: I continue to be amazed by her intelligence, endurance, perseverance, and tenacity after the loss of her husband and the continual presence of diabetes in her life. The only direction she knows is full speed ahead and I've learned more from her than she knows.

Johneese Adams, sister, Fayetteville, Arkansas: a confidante, and one of the most intelligent, talented, and passionate people I know. She's passionate about her family and her work, and she's the hardest working person I've ever known. She deserves more, yet asks for nothing, which has taught me more than she knows.

Rita Oliver, sister, Oklahoma City, Oklahoma: I'm always amazed by her quietness, her dignity, and her gentle spirit. She's persevered through challenges in her life that would have caused a lesser person to withdraw and disappear, and has a wonderful family that displays her legacy.

Mary Horton, sister, Bentonville, Arkansas: the youngest of my five (5) sisters, who has always influenced me with her honesty, her directness, especially with her family, and a humor that keeps those around her, especially her family, from taking themselves too seriously. I've always valued that in her.

Kurt Imel, Wal-Mart District Manger Deceased, Tuscon, Arizona: I refer to Kurt as probably the best manager of people I ever had the honor to supervise, and quite possibly one of the best people I ever knew. He had such a sincere heart for others, yet displayed that heart with objectivity, discipline, passion, and consistency.

How his life came to an end will always be a mystery to me and I had such a great expectation and affection for him that I will feel his loss forever.

Val Robinson, Wal-Mart Store Manager, Aransas Pass, Texas: an individual, who's experienced more setbacks in his life than you could probably say grace over, yet kept coming back over and over again. He influenced me with an ability to move past failure, past disappointment, past bad decisions, past unfairness, past bad luck, past just about any obstacle that came his way, with a sense of optimism, perseverance, and stubbornness that I've yet to find a comparison to. His sense of humor about life, his willingness to take the criticism, and the love he's had for his wife have always been what I've valued the most from knowing him.

Marilyn Terjek, Wal-Mart associate and friend, Las Vegas, Nevada: this lady influenced me with a spirit of friendliness, giving, and caring that is truly significant. I will forever be moved by a gift of rarity that she bestowed simply out of the joy of seeing the pleasure it brought to someone she respected and cared for.

Medina McDade, Re-Max Real Estate associate and friend, Bentonville, Arkansas: One of the few people I know of in my life who made a life-changing decision because of her faith that not many would have had the courage to make. I've always valued her humor, her professionalism, her ability to organize, and her enthusiasm for serving others that has made us kindred spirits.

There are so many more people that deserve to be recognized here and if I'm fortunate enough to be able to author another book, I'll ensure that their names and contributions are included because, though not mentioned at this time, none of them will ever be overlooked. The thing I look forward to the most is being able to add the names and contributions of those who will most assuredly come into my life going forward, because the nature of people and how we live is to continue the process of gathering from those around us that which would enrich our lives, whether in the giving or the receiving.